Neither Socialism nor Monopoly: Theodore Roosevelt and the Decision to Regulate the Railroads

Michael Les Benedict
  The Fruits of Victory: Alternatives in Restoring the Union, 1865-1877

Joseph Boskin
  Into Slavery: Racial Decisions in the Virginia Colony

David M. Chalmers
  Neither Socialism nor Monopoly: Theodore Roosevelt and the Decision to Regulate the Railroads

Roger Daniels
  The Decision to Relocate the Japanese Americans

Richard O. Davies
  The Age of Asphalt: The Automobile, the Freeway, and the Condition of Metropolitan America

Lloyd C. Gardner
  Wilson and Revolutions: 1913-1921

Warren F. Kimball
  Swords or Ploughshares? The Morgenthau Plan for Defeated Nazi Germany, 1943-1946

Ernest R. May
  The Truman Administration and China, 1945-1949

Jane H. and William H. Pease
  The Fugitive Slave Law and Anthony Burns: A Problem in Law Enforcement

J. R. Pole
  The Decision for American Independence

Robert A. Rutland
  Madison's Alternatives: The Jeffersonian Republicans and the Coming of War, 1805-1812

Darrett B. Rutman
  John Winthrop's Decision for America: 1629

Anne F. and Andrew M. Scott
  One Half the People: The Fight for Woman Suffrage

Robert Sobel
  Herbert Hoover at the Onset of the Great Depression, 1929-1930

Theodore Thayer
  Yorktown: Campaign of Strategic Options

Hans L. Trefousse
  Lincoln's Decision for Emancipation

Wilcomb E. Washburn
  The Assault on Indian Tribalism: The General Allotment Law (Dawes Act) of 1887

David M. Chalmers

University of Florida

The America's Alternatives Series ═══════

═══════ Edited by Harold M. Hyman

Neither Socialism nor Monopoly:

Theodore Roosevelt and the Decision to Regulate the Railroads

J. B. Lippincott Company
Philadelphia/New York/San Jose/Toronto

ISBN-0-397-47351-6
Library of Congress Catalog Card Number 75-44355
Printed in the United States of America

1 3 5 7 9 8 6 4 2

Library of Congress Cataloging in Publication Data

Chalmers, David Mark.
  Neither socialism nor monopoly.

  (The America's alternatives series)
  Bibliography: p.
  Includes index.
  1. Railroads and state—United States—History.
2. Roosevelt, Theodore, Pres., U.S., 1858-1919.
I. Title.
HE1051.C4   353.008'75   75-44355
ISBN-0-397-47351-6

FOR KIM AND HENRY
WHO LIKE TRAINS

And with appreciation to Edward Akin, Dwight Alston, Rosemary Brana-Shute, George Crawford Jr., Patrick Delvecchio, Carol Gagnon, Margaret Harris, Joseph Henderson, Marshall Kelley, Patty Lewis, Alan Maclachlan, John Partin, John Spivack, Albert Thorburn, Keith Townsley, Linda Vance, and Harold Wiggins who wrote seminar papers on regulation, to Richard Carnell for letting me read his Yale Senior Essay on Francis G. Newlands, to Norman Wilensky and Jean Chalmers who critically read the manuscript, Steve Kerber who did the polish and proofing and to Harold Hyman who so carefully guided the whole project.

Contents

Foreword ═══════════════════════════════

"When you judge decisions, you have to judge them in the light of what there was available to do it," noted Secretary of State George C. Marshall to the Senate Committees on the Armed Services and Foreign Relations in May 1951.[1] In this spirit, each volume in the "America's Alternatives" series examines the past for insights which History—perhaps only History—is peculiarly fitted to offer. In each volume the author seeks to learn why decision makers in crucial public policy or, more rarely, private choice situations adopted a course and rejected others. Within this context of choices, the author may ask what influence then-existing expert opinion, administrative structures, and budgetary factors exerted in shaping decisions? What weights did constitutions or traditions have? What did men hope for or fear? On what information did they base their decisions? Once a decision was made, how was the decision-maker able to enforce it? What attitudes prevailed toward nationality, race, region, religion, or sex, and how did these attitudes modify results?

We freely ask such questions of the events of our time. This "America's Alternatives" volume transfers appropriate versions of such queries to the past.

In examining those elements that were a part of a crucial historical decision, the author has refrained from making judgment based upon attitudes, information, or values that were not current at the time the decision was made. Instead, as much as possible he or she has explored the past in terms of data and prejudices known to persons contemporary to the event.

1. U.S., Senate, Hearings Before the Committees on the Armed Services and the Foreign Relations of the United States, *The Military Situation in the Far East,* 82d Cong., 2d sess., part I, p. 382. Professor Ernest R. May's "Alternatives" volume directed me to this source and quotation.

Nevertheless, the following reconstruction of one of America's major alternative choices speaks implicitly and frequently, explicitly to present concerns.

In form, this volume consists of a narrative and analytical historical essay (Part One), within which the author has identified by use of headnotes (i.e., Alternative 1, etc.) the choices which he believes were actually before the decision makers with whom he is concerned.

Part Two of this volume contains, in whole or part, the most appropriate source documents that illustrate the Part One Alternatives. The Part Two Documents and Part One essay are keyed for convenient learning use (i.e., the Alternative 1 reference in Part One will contain references to appropriate Part Two Documents). The volume's Part Three offers the user further guidance in the form of a Bibliographical Essay.

Just a century ago, Charles Francis Adams dedicated himself to public service. A son and grandson of United States Presidents, and a Harvard graduate, Adams estimated that Massachusetts' primary problem was to work out acceptable public sector relationships with the increasingly important railroad companies. He accepted the chairmanship of a state planning committee charged with this responsibility. It proved to be difficult, complex, and hard work, and, in the outcome, a failure. Adams was the more irritated, therefore, when, in 1870, he met a touring Illinois legislator, not a college graduate, who was then drafting railroad regulations (to be known as Granger laws) for the midwestern state. Adams remarked how difficult the task was. "Difficult!" the Illinois Granger replied: "Why I don't think I should have any trouble in drawing up an act in half an hour which would settle the whole thing."[2]

The midwesterner's "half an hour" has become a hundred years, and the "whole thing" is still unsettled. Why? Professor Chalmers offers in this volume important ways by which to approach answers to this question. It is increasingly clear that useful answers are still needed for the 1970's, even more urgently than was true in the 1870's.

Harold M. Hyman
Rice University

---

2. Charles Francis Adams, *Remarks on the Subject of a National Railroad Commission, before the Merchants Association of Boston*, (Boston, 1882), p. 4.

Part One

Neither Socialism nor Monopoly

1

Chaos and Power

By 1900, the United States was the world's leading industrial nation, but its governmental structures had not kept pace. Seventy years before, the four-ton, "Best Friend of Charleston," the first commercial locomotive built in America and claimed to be capable of speeds up to twenty miles per hour, made its first scheduled passenger trip—six miles. By 1900, the powerful engines of the New York Central's "Empire State Express" had reached speeds of more than one hundred miles per hour[1] on portions of the 193,000 miles of American railroad.

Already by 1900, the United States had surpassed Britain and Germany in the production of iron, coal, and steel. The railroads, telegraph, and telephone had created a national communication and transportation system which turned the whole country into one vast market. Each city no longer needed its own flour mill and slaughterhouse: people from New York to Los Angeles used flour milled in Minneapolis and beef and pork from the western plains, slaughtered and dressed, canned or refrigerated in Kansas City, Omaha, or Chicago and distributed nationally by the railroads.

The First "Big Business"

The railroads were America's first "big business," and they made other big businesses possible and necessary. They helped open up the western lands for settlement by quickening travel and bringing farm machinery in and crops out. By their own demand for iron, steel, copper, glass, machine tools, and oil, they encouraged the large-scale production that shifted the national unit of manufacture from the blacksmith's forge to the blast furnace. The technology of the Bessemer process and the open hearth, the Westinghouse air brake, the magnificent Pullman Parlor Palace Car, and a thousand other inventions were but part of the response. The width of rails was standardized nationwide at 4 feet, 8½ inches, and local time gave way as trainmen set their big gold watches according to national time zones.

Down on the narrow tip of Manhattan Island, Wall Street developed into a national money market to handle the massive capital needed to build and operate the railroads. The expanding use of corporations, made possible when the states passed general incorporation laws during the 1830s, produced modern accounting and management systems. It also produced the large-scale craft unionism of the Railway Brotherhoods, the industrial unionism of Eugene Debs and the American Railway Union, and the counterresponse of the union-breaking General Managers Association.

A revolution in the scale of enterprise had taken place. Big business reached greater markets than were ever conceived of before and could benefit from the ability to raise vast amounts of capital that made possible the cost

1

economies of large-scale production. It also benefited from the sheer power which made it possible to squeeze out competitors, force down prices paid for labor and raw materials, charge customers more, gain special rates from the railroads, and get special favors and treatment from national and state governments.

To many businessmen, however, this age of industrialization was a chamber of horrors marked by continuous uncertainty, insecurity, and savage economic warfare. The logical goal was to escape through stabilization; the path was consolidation. Out of the expanding market and the drives for security, profits, and power, grew giant corporations such as Standard Oil, American Tobacco, International Harvester, Swift, Armour, and the Carnegie Steel Company.

In the 1870s and 1880s the large corporations had tried to stabilize their situations and their power, by pooling markets and by centralizing management in the hands of trustees, but pooling agreements could not be enforced and state courts found trusts illegal. During the late 1890s and early 1900s, there was a wave of consolidations through new holding companies which were created to own and coordinate multiple companies. Stockholders in smaller companies were either bought out or given shares in the new consolidated companies. This operation took vast amounts of ready money from Wall Street and the banks. With so much money about, those who were arranging things could and did reward themselves richly for their efforts. Stock was issued in amounts considerably larger than the assets of the newly formed holding companies. This meant vast amounts of stock to distribute and to buy and sell on the essentially unregulated stock market, and it meant great profits for insiders who manipulated stock prices. It also meant that the means was available to finance political compaigns and to buy what and whom one needed in government. It meant great power, and it meant that customers would need to be charged high freight rates and prices in order to pay the banks and the bond and stockholders. Some corporations and industries were thus capitalized beyond their capacity to pay their creditors and investors; this in turn made the market and the conomy unstable and price-cutting competition to be even more feared. Such unstable over-expansion, and the continuous ups and downs of the market, helped bring about panics and hard times in the 1870s, 1880s, and most severely in the 1890s.

In his 1904 volume *The Truth About The Trusts*, John Moody, the leading Wall Street authority, identified four hundred and forty-five "active Trusts" made up of more than eight thousand original companies, and capitalized at over twenty billion dollars. Ten of the leading industrial trusts were capitalized at over one hundred million dollars each. In a time when the working man received much less than a thousand dollars a year, Standard Oil had net profits annually in excess of sixty million dollars, which enabled it to spread out into copper, tobacco, gas, banking, insurance, and railroads, as well as in oil and its allied industries.[2]

In 1901, J.P. Morgan, the major Wall Street banker, combined Carnegie and other companies into U.S. Steel, America's first billion dollar corporation. It was a holding company capitalized at approximately 1.4 billion dollars, or about twice the book value of its assets. An estimated 62.5 million dollars went to J.P. Morgan & Company for organizing the combination and handling its stock on the market.[3] This occurred at a time when the value of American manufactures was estimated at some nine billion dollars and government income and expenditures balanced at approximately half a billion dollars a year.

Altogether, the railroads were still the biggest big business. They too were being consolidated into vast holdings. In what were popularly called "communities of interest," the Vanderbilt, Morgan, Harriman, Pennsylvania, Gould, and Rock Island groups would soon control an estimated eighty percent of the nation's railroads, with a capitalization of nine billion dollars. Behind these groups stood the credit of J.P. Morgan & Company, which handled major British investment funds in America, and Kuhn-Loeb & Company, which oversaw the investment of German monies.[4] Bank control and finance capitalism often meant improvement of the roads. It almost certainly meant a vast inflation of railroad indebtedness for which shippers, consumers and, someday, the railroads themselves would have to pay (see Document 1).

Railroad Building: The Railroads, the Courts, and the Congress

American railroad building began in the 1830s. By the outbreak of the Civil War, there were thirty thousand miles of track, two-thirds in the North. Four major trunk lines, the New York Central, the Pennsylvania, the Baltimore & Ohio, and the Erie, pushed their way west to Chicago and the prairies. Within a quarter of a century after the war, the Union Pacific, the Northern Pacific, the Great Northern, the Atchison, Topeka & Santa Fe, the Southern Pacific, and scores of independents and feeder lines crosshatched the western mountains, passes, basins, valleys, and plains. The main grain-carrying, or "granger" lines of the Midwest were the Illinois Central, which had helped Abraham Lincoln make his way as a rising young railroad lawyer, the Rock Island, the Chicago, Burlington & Quincy, the Chicago, Milwaukee & St. Paul, and the Chicago & North Western. In New England the main railroads were the New Haven and the Boston & Maine, while the Louisville & Nashville, the Illinois Central, the Southern, the Seaboard, and the Atlantic Coast Line dominated the South.

Railroad promotion was a national enterprise. Between the 1840s and the 1880s, perhaps more private and public land, monies, and energy went into railroad development than any other enterprise, with the exceptions of westward settlement and the Civil War. If a community were to develop and crops were to get to market, a town or region had to have a railroad; the West had to be "opened up"; passageays to the Pacific had to be built. Much of America's railroad system, unlike Europe's, was built through unoccupied areas, in advance of settlement, and by privately owned companies. Apart from the steamship, the canal, and the oil pipeline, the railroads were the only freight carriers.

Altogether the national government and various states and localities gave some eighty railroads approximately one hundred and eighty million acres of land. This was a territory larger than the prewar German Empire; it was about the size of Texas, or almost seven percent of the continental land area of the nation. In additional grants and bonds, the states provided almost 229 million dollars, the federal government 64.6 million, and municipalities and localities another 300 million, totaling about 600 million dollars turned over to railroads.[5]

However, in the decades of the 1860s, 70s, and 80s, as railroad mileage was doubling and tripling, discontent also grew. Railroad speculation helped produce the panic of 1873 and the bitter depression that followed. In 1877, the railroads twice cut wages, but not dividends; this produced a strike that in places turned into a minor insurrection. Pitched battles were fought, men were killed, and the president sent in the United States Army to retake the nation's rail system from the strikers.

Stock watering, exploitive management, market manipulation, and governmental corruption made millionaires of the Goulds, Vanderbilts, Leland Stanfords, and C.P. Huntingtons. These railroad tycoons also often produced badly built lines and wasted the monies that towns and farmers had invested to create railroad service to their communities. Although freight rates generally declined until the 1900s, agricultural prices also fell. Farmers felt that rates were still too high. More seriously, the railroads gave advantages to one town, commodity, or individual over another, and to the large shipper at the expense of the small. Standard Oil not only got kickbacks, called "rebates," on the oil it shipped, but also forced the railroads to give it part of what its competitors paid as well. Sugar or beef might not pay their fair share of the cost of transportation, so other, less favored, products would have to pay more. Lumber shipped from Texas to Chicago might be charged less than lumber unloaded in Wichita or Emporia, even though they were hundreds of miles closer. Lynchburg, Virginia, might get supplies twice as cheaply as Danville, even though it was farther from the ports and shippers, because it had several railroads and Danville only one. Rates in Georgia or Illinois might be cheaper than rates within Alabama or Wisconsin. The rudeness of the railroads was already legendary, and so was their political power.

The classic textbook story is that the farmers of the old Northwest rose up in the 1870s and organized through the new national Grange of the Patrons of Husbandry to force their legislatures to regulate the railroads. Recent research has established that rather than farmers, those who took the lead in reform movements, were discontented business groups, particularly smaller shippers, such as the commission merchants and other middle men of Milwaukee and Chicago. While the level of rates was important for the farmer and the consumer, equal treatment counted more to the shipper and merchant. For all of them, the prime problem was railroad misbehavior—as they saw it, the "octopus" which lived on the flesh of the yeoman farmer, diligent artisan, and honest merchant.

In 1887, the case of *Munn v. Illinois*,[6] which challenged state regulation of grain warehouses, reached the Supreme Court. In its decision, the Court reasserted the old English common law principle that government could regulate those business which were "affected with the public interest." This public importance, plus the monopolistic nature of the transportation and freight business, justified government intervention. However, many of the "granger" laws emerged from the legislatures too weakened to be very effective. Through propaganda, reductions in service, and outright refusal to obey the new restrictions, the railroads were able to weaken or secure the repeal of these state efforts.

The problems remained. Congressional committees studied and reported. The Senate and House of Representatives each passed bills which the other would not accept because of disagreements over pooling, long-and-short-haul clauses, and whether regulation should be by commission or by the courts. Then, in 1886, the *Wabash* case[7] reached the Supreme Court. Contrary to Illinois law, the Wabash, St. Louis & Pacific Railway charged more to ship goods from the town of Gilman than from Peoria to New York, and Gilman lay between Peoria and New York. The Supreme Court struck down the Illinois law, declaring that the regulation of *interstate* commerce was an exclusive national power. The states could still regulate what was solely within their borders, but commerce between the states was beyond their reach. Interstate control was up to the national government.

After the *Wabash* decision, Congress had to agree on something, and the next year, 1887, an Act to Regulate Commerce became law. A five member Interstate Commerce Commission was established to hear complaints, investigate, issue cease and desist orders, and make damage awards, which would be enforced in the courts. The law required that rates be "just and reasonable," a crucial phrase whose meaning was not defined. All forms of discrimination between persons, places, and kinds of traffic were prohibited, specifically including rebates and other special rates and charges. Rates had to be made public and adhered to, and pooling was prohibited. In response to "long-and-short-haul" complaints, the shorter haul could not be charged more "under substantially similar circumstances and conditions."

Twenty years of demand and the introduction in Congress of some 150 bills had finally produced what was hoped would be the national solution to the "railroad problem" in the form of an independent regulatory commission. The commission was part executive, part legislative, and part judicial. Because of the complexity of rates in a country as large and diverse as the United States, it was not believed possible for fixed standards to be set by Congress. Rather, a commission with members appointed by the president for a fixed term and approved by the Senate would develop the expertise to decide cases and help Congress make general policy concerning the railroads.

The newly born Interstate Commerce Commission began cautiously. Its powers and the "just and reasonable" rates criterion it was to follow were generally undefined, and there were no real precedents as to how such a body should act. What the commission chose to do was to follow the example of the courts, waiting for cases to be brought before it and building up precedents in its solutions to these cases, rather than seeking to guide the railroad industry. It did not see itself as an executive or a planning agency.

Even so, the railroads treated the ICC as an enemy. As the leading historian of commissions, Robert Cushman, summed it up, they "fought, harassed, obstructed, and delayed at every possible point."[8] They disobeyed orders, used every technicality, and withheld evidence which they later presented in appeal to the courts to show that commission decisions had been wrong.

The property conscious, conservative, federal courts badly weakened the commission. Instead of accepting its findings of fact, the courts listened to the evidence which the railroads had held back and, in effect, tried the cases over again. In a series of decisions, the United States Supreme Court decided that the ICC had no power to set a "proper" rate after it had struck down a bad one. The Court also upheld higher freight charges on short hauls, and for a while (until Congress gave it back) it took away the ICC's power to compel witnesses to give testimony. While the Court did not deny that Congress had the right to establish such a commission, it took a broad view of what was a "fair return" for the railroads and a very narrow view of the powers of the ICC. With diminished powers and prestige, buffeted by the railroads, and with its decisions winding slowly through the courts on their way to probable reversals, by 1900 the nation's first independent regulatory commission would have to be written down as a failure.

Notes

1. John F. Stover, *The Life and Decline of the American Railroad* (New York: Oxford University Press, 1970), pp. 11, 78.

2. John Moody, *The Truth About the Trusts* (New York: Moody Publishing Co., 1904), pp. 488-93.

3. Ibid., pp. 133-204; Harold U. Faulkner, *The Decline of Laissez-Faire* (New York: Rinehart Co., 1951), p. 161.

4. Faulkner, *The Decline of Laissez-Faire*, pp. 191-202.

5. William Z. Ripley, *Railroads: Rates and Regulation* (New York: Longreaves, Green, & Co., 1912), pp. 35-43; D. Philip Locklin, *Economics of Transportation* (Homewood, Ill.: R.D. Irwin, 1966), pp. 101-16; John F. Stover, *American Railroads* (Chicago: University of Chicago Press, 1961), pp. 87-92. At least the national government's investment was repaid with interest in the case of the bonds, and by special government rates in return for the land grants.

6. *Munn v. Illinois*, 94 U.S. 113 (1877).

7. *Wabash, St. Louis and Pacific Railway Company v. Illinois*, 118 U.S. 557 (1886).

8. Robert E. Cushman, *The Independent Regulatory Commissions* (New York: Oxford University Press, 1941), p. 66.

2

Alternatives

The Railroad Problem

By 1900, the independent commission to regulate the railroads seemed to be a failure. What was to be done—if anything really needed to be done at all? What were the alternatives? The widespread popular and political feeling was that some action indeed was necessary. Throughout the world of railroads, as in business generally, a massive consolidation was taking place. As the prime railroad authority, Harvard Professor William Z. Ripley, commented, "many small local roads, long closely identified with the welfare of particular communities, were now merged in great systems under entirely different and probably absentee ownership and management. Boston, Baltimore, New Orleans, St. Paul, Cincinnati, not to mention a host of other smaller places, seemed commercially cast adrift." [1]

At the same time, freight rates, which has been declining since the 1870s, now rose steadily. This was directly seen as the result of the growing combinations and the replacement of competition by financial control. The public attention focused on the power of a few men such as the railroad magnate E.H. Harriman, the oil monopolist John D. Rockefeller, and the banker J.P. Morgan as symbols of concentrated economic power. The newspapers were full of stories of the misdeeds of the "trusts" and their "masters." The serious, highbrow magazines, such as the *North American Review*, debated the topics of national regulation and government ownership.

In the world of the new, lively, inexpensive popular magazines such as *McClure's*, *Everybody's*, *Collier's*, and *Cosmopolitan*, a new breed of journalists arose, whom Theodore Roosevelt was to label "muckrakers." They focused on the malevolent effects of what they variously called "Big Business," "the Interests," "the System," "plutocracy," "Frenzied Finance," "Trusts," and "Monopoly." In almost every case, whether it was Ida Tarbell writing the "History of the Standard Oil Company," or Charles Edward Russell holding forth on the Beef Trust which three times a day came to the table of "every household in America," favoritism in transportation lay at the hear of monopoly power. In a series titled "Railroads on Trial," the muckraker Ray Stannard Baker typically saw himself leading a crusade against special privilege, whose heart was the power of the railroads.

In 1903 the railroads themselves, with much self-congratulation, sponsored the Elkins Act. Its purpose was to prevent the loss of revenue that came from rebates and special favors, but this, along with an Expediting Act to speed ICC cases through the courts, was not enough. The railroad "problem" or "scandal"—depending on one's perspective—had become a major national issue. An activist president, Theodore Roosevelt, decided to do something.

What were the alternatives? (see Document 2).

Alternative 1: Return to competition. Seek low freight rates by attacking monopolistic arrangements, restraints of trade (including favoritism) through use of a strengthened antitrust law.

Alternative 2: No regulation. Let the market function unhampered. This would mean the survival of the best and most efficient units, including consolidated railroad systems. Cutthroat competition, pooling, mergers, or any form of consolidation which the market produced would be legal. Presumably monopoly profits would either lead to competition from new entrants or to an efficient, stable, consolidated system.

Alternative 3: Regulation by the states. Since the states were smaller, closer, and potentially more responsive to the popular will than the national government, they would be more likely to be innovative and concerned about the public interest.

Alternative 4: Extensive national regulation. Supervision of physical evaluation, capitalization, minimum as well as maximum rates, rate-setting, labor, and safety conditions could be achieved either through a greatly strengthened commission or by the national incorporation and consolidation of the railroads.

Alternative 5: Government ownership. Socialism with or without the socialist state, following such models of national ownership of railroads as Germany, Switzerland, New Zealand, Australia, Japan, and an increasing number of other countries, might be the best solution to the railroad problem.

Alternative 6: Improved commission regulation. A strengthened ICC might control maximum and discriminatory rates, thus preventing rebates and other forms of favoritism.

Return to Competition

Was a return to competition (*Alternative 1*) possible? The rise of the giant corporation and the railroad empire was a new development no more than a quarter of a century old. It ran against the American national self-image. Americans had traditionally seen themselves as a nation of farmers, mechanics, merchants, and small businessmen—a country without great landed estates or an hereditary aristocracy standing in the way of opportunity for all. In what was still a nation of family farms, the governing images were those of the independent yeomen, Andrew Jackson's struggle against the seond Bank of the United States, and a Civil War-bred image of Abraham Lincoln standing firm against a slaveowning, plantation South.

The sudden shift from small to giant enterprise created problems of psychological as well as political and economic adjustment. Giant business meant a threat to political equalitarianism. The likelihood that great wealth might mean rule by a corrupt plutocracy seemed to be borne out by the stories that filled the press and magazines. How could a free people survive a world of giant business and monopoly? The dominant economic theory was the classicial model of competition: competition would make the best distribution of resources, produce the goods, improve the quality of the goods and their technology, pay the best price for labor and raw materials, and keep down the cost to consumers. At the same time, it would preserve the nation's free institutions and the spirit of enterprise and equality.

In 1890, Congress had overwhelmingly passed the Sherman Antitrust Act to protect free enterprise in America by prohibiting any "conspiracy in restraint of trade." Although only five years later in the "Sugar Trust Case" *(U.S. v. E.C. Knight)* the Supreme Court distinguished between manufacture and commerce and let monopoly control of refining stand, but railroads were clearly commerce and fell within the scope of the act. Even the Supreme Court felt obliged in 1897 to strike down the gigantic Trans-Missouri Freight Association,[2] which set rates on the western railroads, as a violation of the Sherman Act.

Antitrust law has alternately been seen as a way to preserve a society of small competitive units without market power, and as a way to discipline large corporations which used market power improperly against competitors and consumers. The twentieth-century history of antitrust has been a story of both usages. Theodore Roosevelt, who had no animosity against bigness per se, was willing to use the Sherman Act to punish misbehavior. "The most powerful men in this country were held to accountability before the law," he boasted.[3] The Sherman Act was one way to make powerful men answerable to society, and there were not many other instruments at hand. When the railroad monarchs E.H. Harriman and James J. Hill (with the support of their respective banking houses of Kuhn, Loeb and J.P. Morgan) resolved a battle for possession of the Chicago, Burlington & Quincy by putting the northwestern railroads into one great holding company, Roosevelt brought suit and in 1904 won the Northern Securities case in the Supreme Court *(Alternative 1:* Document 3). He and his successor, William Howard Taft, who had studied at Yale under the high priest of the competition-minded economists, William Graham Sumner, launched other antitrust suits against such giants as Swift, Standard Oil, American Tobacco, and U.S. Steel.

Here was a means by which railroad collusion and consolidation, price-fixing, rebating, and other misdeeds might be prevented. Perhaps the Supreme Court could be weaned away from blunting antitrust prosecutions and thus provide what the economy and society needed. Perhaps if what constituted a "restraint of trade" were made more specific, as Woodrow Wilson tried to do in 1914 with the Clayton Act, business, government, and the courts would all know better what was expected of them.

While antitrust activity has sometimes rested, as it did during the 1920s and the first part of Franklin Roosevelt's New Deal, it has always emerged again. Despite all the reasons and experience to the contrary, antimonopoly and a belief in price determination in the marketplace—rather than in the board room or the country club—have persisted in America. In the latter part of the New Deal, FDR turned to antitrust in the hope of stimulating the economy by lowering prices. Despite Richard Nixon's "expletive deleted" remarks about anti-trust prosecutions, two Republican presidents looked to antitrust and the Federal Trade Commission during the 1970s to try to break a persisting inflation which had injured the vitality of the economy. From Theodore Roosevelt's Northern Securities prosecution in 1902 to Gerald Ford's case against American Telegraph & Telephone in 1974, antitrust has remained a possible means to economic well-being which the American government and people have never been quite willing either comprehensively to use or completely to abandon.

Laissez-Faire

Was laissez-faire (*Alternative 2*) possible? To fully achieve this would have meant no government regulation. Within the business and financial community there were those who opposed any meaningful regulation, and there were economists and United States Senators who agreed with them. One of the most important national attitudes, rising out of a persisting American individualism, has been a distrust of government. By the end of the nineteenth century, this feeling had been combined with the "laws" of supply and demand and Herbert Spencer's "survival of the fittest" social darwinism to form an economic and social philosophy. Much of American conservatism was being converted from belief in an organic society of settled, traditional relations, to belief in a society whose relationships were contractual ones, set in the marketplace. A property-oriented legal profession and judiciary tended to equate limitations on profits, as well as almost any regulatory restruction, with a denial of due process. At the same time, many of the same businessmen and lawyers did not object to governmental subsidies, land-grants, loans, the gold standard, antiunion policies, and even the protective tariff. What they meant by laissez-faire was no government *regulation* of business. To many, a regulatory government—state or national—was contrary to the laws of economics, the Constitution, society, American individualism, basic morality, and human nature.

The nineteenth-century leaders studied by the economic historian Thomas Cochran opposed regulation on two major grounds: the inefficiency and corruption of politicians, and the belief that regulation could do no positive good. James C. Clarke, president of the New Haven Railroad, characterized would-be regulators as "demagogues, politicians and communists." While the president of the Chicago, Burlington & Quincy wrote that "there was never anything more absurd and ridiculous than that prosperity can be brought to a country by legislation."[4]

Not all railroad executives, businessmen, and bankers opposed regulation. A significant number, such as steel-maker Andrew Carnegie, International Harvester magnate George Perkins, and Pennsylvania Railroad President Alexander Cassatt supported Theodore Roosevelt's efforts. Able present-day "New Left" historians argue that regulation was really the instrument by which businessmen tried to use government to build monopolistic or cartel-like arrangements that they could not nail down in the market. The historian Gabriel Kolko calls this strategy "political capitalism."[5] However, many railroad leaders, lawyers, businessmen and bankers did oppose governmental regulation. For the government to set rates was "confiscatory" and therefore "unconstitutional." If government was to have a hand in it, establishing standards was a legislative or judicial responsibility; for Congress to delegate it to a commission was unconstitutional. Conservatives believed that only the courts had the constitutional right to decide whether any specific railroad rate was "unreasonable"; it would be unconstitutional for a commission to make that decision. These were questions which seriously worried many constitutional lawyers and lawyer-senators such as Philander C. Knox, formerly Theodore Roosevelt's attorney general, and, in 1906, senator from Pennsylvania. Businessmen-senators such as the wealthy Republican leader from Rhode Island, Nelson W. Aldrich, whose daughter had married John D. Rockefeller, Jr., simply did not like anything that interferred with business and business wealth (*Alternative 2:* see Document 4).

When the Senate held hearings on the question during the summer of 1905, railroad leaders rallied public opinion against a railroad bill. Witnesses before the Senate committee, chaired by wealthy railroad owner Stephen B. Elkins, argued that:

1) Government-set rates would impede industrial progress.
2) The government was not capable of handling thousands of commodities, rates, and situations on the nation's two hundred thousand miles of railroads.
3) Railroad rate-making by government would mean that political considerations and influence would be corruptly substituted for market judgments.
4) Regulation would drive away investors.
5) The men who owned the railroads had the right to run them.
6) Whatever balancing and adjustments were necessary could best take place in the market.[6]

But although there was much talk about the market, few maintained that laissez-faire would mean competition. The classical definition of competition as a large number of small firms, no one or group of which had any control over price, certainly did not describe the railroads. Despite common law antimonopoly principles and state and national regulatory efforts, the American railroad system was highly consolidated. One of the major forces behind this phenomenon had been the desire to escape from competition. The greatest consolidator, J.P. Morgan, hated competition. Its rate wars wasted investors' funds, cut profits, and drove railroads to bankruptcy.

From the beginning railroad men had combined, as Adam Smith had warned that "people in the same trade" were likely to do. Voluntary division of traffic in the form of pools, however, did not work well. Someone always undercut the pool, and the Interstate Commerce Act of 1887, passed after much debate, made pooling illegal. But there were other means to achieve the same goal. The railroad industry obviously needed some sort of governance, and the bankers were developing one. In the 1880s, J.P. Morgan became the prime initiator of internally developed and self-imposed rules. A rate war between the New York Central and the Pennsylvania was cutting dividends.

Each was threatening to invade the other's territory. Morgan invited the two railroad presidents to a meeting on his yacht *Corsair* and kept them apparently willing prisoners until they worked out a mutually agreeable solution. Particularly after the bitter panic and depression of the 1890s, the bankers took the lead in reorganizing and consolidating railroads.

Titans such as E.H. Harriman, who controlled the Southern and Union Pacific Railroads, and Morgan's partner James J. Hill of the Northern Pacific and Great Northern, battled and then consolidated, though President Roosevelt, the Sherman Act, and the Supreme Court knocked out that particular arrangement. As the United States Industrial Commission reported after the turn of the century, eighty percent of the nation's railroad mileage was concentrated in the hands of such "communities of interest" (see Document 1). The most dynamic of the bank-backed magnates was Harriman, who had dreams of stretching his railroad empire across Asia as well as America. Answering a Senate Committee question in December of 1906 as to when he would have enough, he replied that he would "go on" as long as life and the law would let him.[7]

In his highly popular textbook of 1889, Harvard economist David Ames Wells wrote that to prevent industrial concentrations and combinations was to war against progress and civilization. "The world demands abundance of commodities, and demands them cheaply; and experience shows that it can have them only by the employment of great capital upon the most extensive scale."[8]

Magnates such as Morgan, Harriman, and Hill were willing to undertake the responsibility and the power of private government. The Great Northern's president testified contemptuously to the Elkins Committee in 1905 that none of the ICC Commissioners could have earned their pay in railroad management (*Alternative 2*: see Document 5). As Roosevelt himself musingly recognized, Morgan considered the United States government as a rival concentrate, with which—if necessary—he was willing to work out a greater community of interest.[9]

Another present-day railroad historian, Albro Martin, argues eloquently that what most damaged the railroads was atomistic competition in the nineteenth century and government regulation that starved capital formation and the spirit of enterprise in the twentieth. With praise of pooling and condemnation of regulation in his 1971 prize-winning *Enterprise Denied*, Martin seemed to be casting his belated vote for the private governance of the railroads. During the Progressive Era, both Harriman and Morgan were aggressively ready to consolidate the nation's railroads into their own privately owned empires.

Regulation by the States

Was regulation by the states (*Alternative 3*) possible? Modern New Left critics have sought a more democratic alternative to the national bureaucratization of modern "liberalism," which they see as a captive to economic interest. In the early twentieth century, the possible role of the individual states in economic regulation seemed more promising than it does today. In the 1900s, it was the national government that was sluggishly conservative and the states that were often much more experimental, especially in the Midwest. While Standard Oil was doing everything to the legislature of Pennsylvania, according to the old wheeze, "except refine it," Ohio indicated the trust and Missouri fought to prevent it from doing business within that state. Most states had some form of railroad commission, and those of the Midwest showed muscle.

By 1902, thirty-one of the forty-five states had railroad commissions. The first big wave of regulation had been the "granger laws"during the 1870s in states such as Wisconsin, Illinois, and Minnesota. However, those state laws not overturned by the courts, were usually modified or repealed through the railroads' influence. Although in the 1886 *Wabash* case the Supreme Court gave sole control over interstate commerce to the national government, the states could still regulate railroad operations which were entirely within their boundaries. During the turbulent 1890s, and on into the 1900s, many states tried strong regulation, usually through commissions which were given power over corporations and public utilities as well. Particularly in the South and Midwest the commissions were given rate—making powers and were some-times directed to develop complete statewide rate systems, controlling minimum as well as maximum rates, costs of construction, physical valuation and taxation of railroads, and supervision of finances.

In Alabama, the railroads emerged as the prime political issue as Braxton Bragg Comer battled his way to the governorship through his promise to wring a two-cents per mile fare—"just like folks are charged in Georgia"—out of Milton Hannibal Smith's Louisville & Nashville Railroad. In Wisconsin, Robert M. La Follette similarly fought his way to political power by opposing the railroad-lumber-corporation combination that ran the state Republican party and the legislature. Along with his struggle for primary elections, La Follette campaigned on the promise to evaluate, tax, and regulate the Chicago, Milwaukee & St. Paul and the Chicago and North Western railroads (*Alternative 3:* see Document 6).

Working with La Follette was Tax Commissioner Nils Haugen, an overt antagonist of the railroads, who had once written to the president of the Chicago, Milwaukee & St. Paul: "If I have any prejudices against railway management it grows largely out of the fact that I have had a slight peek behind the curtain."[10] Well might the latterday critic Gabriel Kolko quote the letter from a "harried railroad man" to the ICC who wrote, "Oh Lord pity us in Neb. and preserve us from the results of a populist legislature and State government," to support the proposition that the railroads looked to the national government for protection from the states.[11]

In time, the states would turn out not to be very fearful. The commissioners, such as those in Wisconsin, were often passive and timid, while the courts struck down strong regulatory efforts in Alabama and Minnesota. In sum, the courts were generally hostile to meaningful state regulation. State railroad commissioners were usually "cooperative" or unventuresome, and commissions became allies rather than regulators. The railroads came to see the commissions as shields, rather than as threats to their economic well-being.

Strong National Regulation

Many people saw strong national regulation (*Alternative 4*) as the proper way to deal with the railroads. La Follette, the Republican senator from Wisconsin, and Francis G. Newlands, the Democratic senator from Nevada, offered plans. "I do not believe government ownership either the necessary or the best solution of the transportation problem as it exists in the United States to-day," La Follette told the Senate in a three-day speech during the debate on the Hepburn Act. "But, as I trust I have made clear," he went on, "for my whole argument is based on that premise, I believe that the Government of the United States is bound to exercise all the power of a sovereign nation to the end that the regulation and control of its commerce shall be just and equitable, not only to shippers, but to the whole public. It is bound to see to it that the country is not handed over to monopoly and to selfish interests." [12]

La Follette, newly arrived in the Senate after having forced through a comprehensive railroad bill in Wisconsin, believed that national regulation should seek three goals:
1) To prevent "unjust and extortionate rates,"
2) To prevent discrimination between shippers, localities, or commodities, and
3) To enforce adequate service.

The problem with the Hepburn bill, which the Senate came to consider in 1906, was that it was solely and inadequately concerned with discrimination. La Follette believed that the bill aided the large shippers who did not care how high the rates were, as long as no one got better ones.

La Follette had been consumer-oriented in Wisconsin as well as Washington. He felt that high rates forced up the costs of living, and that unwarranted increases, passed on to the consumers, were mounting to at least one hundred million dollars a year. La Follette sought to give the ICC power to fix all rates, minimum as well as maximum, and to prevent discriminations and market favoritism. He believed that it was necessary to have railroad property evaluated in order to determine fair rates, and that these rates should be set by the replacement value of the railroads, excluding the inflated costs of original construction and the often-watered stocks and bonds. Imprisonment for violations, which had been eliminated by the Elkins anti-rebate law of 1903, needed to be restored (*Alternative 4:* see Document 7).

When the journalist Lincoln Steffens arranged a meeting between La Follette and Theodore Roosevelt, the senator soon discovered that the president was really seeking only to prevent discrimination. This, Roosevelt believed, was a proper step-by-step approach and all that the country was ready for. La Follette disagreed. It was better to seek what was necessary, endure temporary defeat, educate the people, and come back fighting. Roosevelt, he complained, was too willing to settle for half-a-loaf.[13]

If "Fighting Bob" La Follette saw the problem of the railroads as one of democracy and the struggle against "the interests," Francis G. Newlands, the Nevada Democrat, approached it from the viewpoint of efficiency. He was alarmed by monopoly, "the evils of overcapitalization," stock speculation, political corruption, and industrial accidents. He was also impressed by the fact that the forty-five different states and the national government each had its own franchise, valuation, tax, and regulatory systems. The possiblities of corruption between the two thousand railroad corporations and the thousands of local officials who manned the various governmental systems, were immense. Unless the railroad system was unified and simplified, the complexity of the situation would drive the country to government ownership. Such a step might provide many benefits, but there were still the "possible evils" of bureaucracy, unbusinesslike methods, and political patronage. The alternative solution was to recognize that railroad transportation was a natural monopoly and treat it as such.

Newlands had risen from poverty to great wealth, marrying the daughter of one of the richest men in California and eventually inheriting the fabulous Comstock mine in Nevada. Along the way, he moved from financial buccaneering to social concern and constructive politics. He focused his own efforts on rational and systematic planning. Within Congress he was a spokesman of the new, rising cult of professional management and efficiency, which had especially invaded the field of natural resources. Newlands himself had pushed the National Reclamation Act of 1902, called the Newlands Act, to consolidate control over irrigation in the West.

He presented to Congress and expounded in magazine articles and debates a program of a national incorporation and consolidation for the railroads. Under a unified and simplified system, capitalization could be brought into correspondence with valuation, and a secure return of at least four percent could be permitted. The railroads would be exempt from all but a single tax on gross receipts, gradually increasing to five percent. This would be collected by the national government and largely distributed to the states, thus ending the need—and cost—of political corruption in the states. With enhanced rationality and efficiency, more money would go to the states and more would be available for higher railroad wages and shorter working hours, and for sickness and old age pensions for labor. All labor and accident disputes would be handled through arbitration. By this plan, Senator Newlands proudly claimed, the country might gain "nearly all of the benefits of Government ownership, with none of its dangers." (*Alternative 4:* see Document 9).

Government Ownership

Although it lacked supporters in the United States Senate, government ownership (*Alternative 5*) seemed to many people to be the proper solution to the railroad problem. The subject was probably much more widely discussed in the 1900s than it was to be in the 1970s as government backed into increasing control of the nation's rail network.

At the beginning of the twentieth century, as in the present decade, the dominant pattern of railroad relationships to government authority pattern was public ownership. The leading example of public service and efficiency was the imperial German system, but the experiences of Switzerland, Belgium, Denmark, Australia, and New Zealand were also discussed in America by politicians and in the press. There was also much interest in the mixed systems of private and public ownership and public regulation in England and Canada. Critics such as Chicago economist Hugo B. Meyer and "old guard" senators Henry Cabot Lodge and Joseph Foraker pointed out that American rates were lower than those in other countries. La Follette responded by praising the German state-owned railroads as being public and service oriented, while American railroading was marked by discrimination, a lack of concern for safety for passengers and workers, and greed.[14]

With the growing consolidation of big business and the expansion of municipally owned utility systems, many people saw nationalization as the wave of the future. The leaders of the Socialist Party of America, formed in 1901, the same year as United States Steel was incorporated, believed that the railroads would inevitably be removed from the exploitive hands of private ownership. However, other than their attack on railroad abuses and alleged capitalist oppression, socialists contributed relatively little to the debate. The conservative Milwaukee socialist Victor Berger and the militant Eugene Debs disagreed over whether nationalization under capitalism would do much good, but neither presented concrete short-range programs for the period prior to the arrival of "collective ownership and the democratic management of the railroads" under socialism.[15]

However, many reform and socialist-minded writers and intellectuals had a great deal to say. The lawyer, civil engineer, and Boston University professor Frank Parsons numbered mayors, labor leaders, social workers, ministers, and professors as officers of his National League for Promoting Public Ownship of Monopolies. Among them were the mayors of Denver, Des Moines, Toledo, Columbus, and Duluth, Michigan Governor Hazen S. Pingree, clergymen Washington Gladden, Charles M. Sheldon and Russell H. Conwell, social workers and women's rights leaders Jane Addams, Elizabeth Cady Stanton, Frances Williard, Dr. Anna Shaw, and Charlotte Perkins Stetson (Gilman), professors John R. Commons and J. Allen Smith, editor and literary critic William Dean Howells, and labor leader Samuel Gompers.[16]

Through articles, particularly in B.O. Flowers's public ownership-minded magazine, *The Arena*, and in books, and legislative testimony, Parsons was the outstanding spokesman for nationalization. In debate that ranged widely but drawing particularly from the German experience, he maintained that low American rates were the product of much longer (and therefore cheaper) freight hauls and did not reveal the great variations and ills done by discriminations. Basically, he argued, rates would decrease under state control in the United States, as they had done abroad. Private monopoly sought dividends, while public ownership aimed at service. Nationalization would mean lower costs from the one great consolidation, and no more corruption funds, rebates or other forms of discrimination, secret commissions, passes, or watered stock. Long before the British economist John Maynard Keynes began urging governments to spend their way out of depressions, Parsons pointed out to the Industrial Commission the examples of Germany and New Zealand, where government railroad building helped the economy during hard times while slackening off in prosperity periods, in a way directly contrary to the American pattern under private ownership. "We do not run the roads to make money," he quoted the head of the railroad commission in Australia's New South Wales, "but for the convenience of the public and the good of men." (*Alternative 5:* see Document 10).

In an important series during the 1906 Senate debate on railroad legislation, the noted journalist Charles Edward Russell, well along the path toward joining the Socialist party, described the benefits of public ownership around the world:

> "so far as any outsider can discover there is no grafting—and assuredly there is no stock juggling, no bond juggling, rate juggling, rebates, discriminations, thefts, underbilling, wrong classifications, skin games, and frauds on shippers. . . .lobbies, pools, combinations, dark-lantern deals, secret compacts, crooked Congressmen, purchased Senators, Bribed District Attorneys."

So it was across the globe. In discussing the experience of western Australia, he wrote "President Roosevelt could never persuade the people. . .that the government ownership of railroads is the greatest misfortune that can befall a nation."[17]

Improved Commission Regulation

However, that was exactly what President Theodore Roosevelt believed. In attempting to improve commission regulation (*Alternative 6*) by strengthening the ICC, Roosevelt sought to curb the "greed" of corrupt magnates that was stirring up the "unwise" public clamor for socialism. Roosevelt's widely popular path was to avoid extreme or comprehensive solutions to the problem of big business, and particularly transportation. He considered the railroads to be a crucial concern, and in a not uncharacteristically American way, he sought a middle solution.

For the president, the need to strengthen the ICC was great from a practical standpoint, as well as to cut off rising sentiment for a more radical, socialist alternative. Of course, it would have been possible to do nothing. If the lawyers, railroad presidents, and senators who opposed reform were successful, this would have been the result—at least for the time being. However, leaving things the way they were hardly seemed a solution to anyone. The existing degree of regulation, combined with occasional antitrust onslaughts, meant few gains for shippers and consumers, and uncertainty for the railroads. Rebates and discriminations would continue, rates and prices would rise, and the railroads would not be able to find a dependable, consistent state either of competition or consolidation. It seemed clear and pressing that something be done.

Notes

1. William Z. Ripley, *Railroads: Rates and Regulations* (New York: Longreaves, Green & Co., 1912), pp. 487-88.

2. *United States v. E.C. Knight Company,* 156 U.S. 1 (1895); *United States v. Trans-Missippi Freight Association,* 166 U.S. 290 (1897).

3. Richard Hofstadter, *The Paranoid Style in American Politics and Other Essays* (New York: Alfred A. Knopf, 1965), p. 203.

4. Thomas C. Cochran, *Railroad Leaders, 1845-1890* (Cambridge, Mass.: Harvard University Press, 1953), pp. 189-90.

5. Gabriel Kolko, *The Triumph of Conservatism* (New York: Free Press of Glencoe, 1963).

6. U.S., Congress, Senate, Committee on Interstate Commerce, *Hearings on the Regulation of Railway Rates,* 59th Cong., 1st sess., 1906, vol. 1, pp. 120-26.

7. Quoted in Ripley, *Railroads,* pp. 490-91.

8. Quoted by Nicholas Katzenbach in *The Future of Capitalism,* National Industrial Conference Board (New York; Macmillan Co., 1967), pp. 111-12.

9. Joseph Bishop, *Theodore Roosevelt and His Time, Shown in His Own Letters* (New York: Charles Scribner's Sons, 1920), vol. 1, pp. 184-85.

10. Quoted in Stanley P. Caine, *The Myth of a Progressive Reform: Railroad Regulation in Wisconsin* (Madison: State Historical Society of Wisconsin, 1970), p. 125.

11. Gabriel Kolko, *Railroads and Regulation, 1877-1916* (Princeton: Princeton University Press, 1965), p. 164.

12. U.S., Congress, Senate, *Congressional Record,* 59th Cong., 1st sess., 1906, vol. 40, pt. 6, p. 5705.

13. *La Follette's Autobiography* (Madison: University of Wisconsin Press, 1960 ed.), pp. 174-75.

14. *Congressional Record,* 59th Cong., 1st sess., 1906, vol. 40, pt. 6, pp. 5702-5.

15. Morris Hillquit, *Socialism Summed Up* (New York: H.K. Fly Co., 1913), p. 71.

16. U.S., Congress, Senate, U.S. Industrial Commission, *Report: Testimony to the Commission,* 57th Cong., 1st sess., 1902, vol. 9, pp. 168-69.

17 Quoted in David Chalmers, *The Muckrake Years* (New York: Van Nostrand Reinhold Co., 1974), pp. 116, 118.

3

The Battle for the Hepburn Act of 1906

Roosevelt Enters the Fight

The battle for Theodore Roosevelt's middle-of-the-road alternative of strengthening the Interstate Commerce Commission was fought in the Senate of the United States during the spring of 1906. But while the senators debated, probably changing no votes in that chamber, the crucial marshalling of forces went on its cloakrooms and in the White House. No United States senator is likely to be without a position on so important an issue, but the master antagonists were President Roosevelt and the majority leader of his party, Rhode Island's Senator Nelson W. Aldrich.

It was an exciting contest and one told well by the historians, particularly by John Blum, who helped edit the Roosevelt letters, and William Harbaugh, who has written the best Roosevelt biography.[1] They and the other historians of the era have pieced together the evidence and made good guesses, but one insight which still eludes us is a look into the inner depths of Nelson W. Aldrich. He had worked his way up from modest beginnings in the grocery business, through civic affairs and politics in the controlled Republican fiefdom of Rhode Island, to wealth and leadership in the United States Senate. John D. Rockefeller, Jr., married his daughter. His grandson and namesake, Nelson W. Rockefeller, was to be governor of New York and vice president of the United States. It does not seem that anyone bought Aldrich's vote; it belonged only to him, and he had his convictions. Disdainful of the powerless and of lesser mortals, he identified the interests of the nation with the possessors of wealth and power, who often returned the courtesy.

With William McKinley's "Gold Standard" victory over William Jennings Bryan in the election of 1896, the Republicans had firmly become the majority party of the nation. In the Congress, party cohesiveness was growing and the leadership was strong. While the vituperative proponent of high tariffs, Speaker Joe Cannon, directed the affairs of the House of Representatives, Aldrich and his "old guard" faction dominated the Senate. Through their power in the party caucus and its steering committee, on committee assignments, and on the Appropriations, Finance, Commerce, and Rules committees, they ran the business of the Senate.[2]

Theodore Roosevelt was not a revolutionary; he was a politician and a superb one. His task was to work within a conservative system and a conservative party. But unchecked corporate power was a problem and there were stirrings in the country and among the party's midwestern representatives. The president read the signs, and inactivity was not congenial to his nature.

In December, 1904, he lamented to his close friend C.A. Spring Rice, the future British ambassador, "a well-defined opinion is growing up among the people at large that the Republican party has become unduly subservient to the so-called Wall Street men—to the men of mere wealth, the plutocracy; and of all possible oligarchies I think an oligarchy of colossal capitalists is the most narrow-minded and the meanest in its ideals."[3] The following spring he commented further to the great British historian George Otto Trevelyan that "somehow or other we shall have to work out methods of controlling the big corporations without paralyzing the energies of the business community and of preventing any tyranny on the part of the labor unions. . . ." In this, he went on, he had "just as much difficulty in preventing the demagogues from going too far as in making those who are directly or indirectly responsive to Wall Street go far enough" (see Documents 12 and 13).[4]

In his December, 1904, State of the Union message to Congress, Roosevelt spoke at length of the need for evenhanded national regulation of great corporations. "Above all else," he stated, "we must strive to keep the highways of commerce open to all on equal terms."[5] The next year, control of corporations and railroad regulation had moved up to the leading place in his message and he devoted more pages to them, calling further railroad regulation "the immediate and most pressing need" of the Congress. This time, he stated specifically that he wanted to strengthen the Interstate Commerce Commission so that it could act with speed and force to prevent unfair or discriminatory rates or other charges and arrangements. "The question of transportation," he said, "lies at the root of all industrial success" (*Alternative 6*: see Document 11).

The president's 1904 call for comprehensive legislation came on the heels of his sweeping election victory, but he and his cautious advisors did not get a bill on the floor of the Senate until the spring of 1906. That it got even that far was something of a tribute to Roosevelt's political skill. The Roosevelt historian John Blum offers a convincing thesis that the president maneuvered the Republican old guard in both Houses into permitting his railroad bill to reach the floor by frightening them with a threatened downward revision of the tariff. Conservative legislators, fearing that such reductions would open the American market to competition from abroad, apparently yielded some ground to the president's carefully orchestrated campaign. A new railroad law would at least be considered.[6]

Important accomplishments sometimes come in small steps. Roosevelt had had little interest in tariff revision, but he believed the railroad problem to be crucial. In writing to his friend, the influential Protestant theologian and editor Lyman Abbott, he stated that "on the interstate commerce business, which I regard as a matter of principle, I shall fight. On the tariff, which I regard as a matter of expediency, I shall endeavor to get the best results I can, but I shall not break with my party."[7]

A railroad bill easily passed the House of Representatives, but the Senate was not yet ready for this step, and the bill died in the Commerce Committee. However, that committee, chaired by the West Virginia coal and railroad millionaire, Stephen Elkins, agreed to hold full hearings on railroad regulation. Over the summer of 1905, the committee produced five volumes of testimony. Meanwhile, Roosevelt alternated between frightening the old guard on the tariff and using his travels in the West and South to build up sentiment for railroad regulation.

The Struggle in Committee and in the Senate

If it was a matter of "principle" for Theodore Roosevelt, railroad regulation had become close to a moral crusade for many, such as the able Republican senator from Iowa, Jonathan Dolliver (see Document 14). To them it seemed to be a contest between "the Great Republic and the Money Power," which reached the level of the previous generation's struggle over slavery. The railroad regulation bill, introduced by Iowa Congressman Peter Hepburn, swept through the House with only seven dissenting votes and went to the Senate Commerce Committee. Perhaps the pressures in the country and the commitment in the House of Representatives were too strong to stem the tide there. Perhaps it was the president's tariff trade-off with House Speaker "Uncle Joe" Cannon that moved the bill so swiftly. At any rate, everybody knew that the real battle would be in the Senate. In that body, there were fifty-seven Republicans and thirty-three Democrats (with Oklahoma, Arizona, New Mexico, Alaska, and Hawaii not yet states). The growing popular pressure for railroad regulation had deprived Aldrich of some of his formerly staunch midwestern allies, such as Iowa Senator William Allison and Wisconsin's John Spooner. Although reformist sentiment was rising among midwestern Republicans who would soon be calling themselves "Progressives," the Senate was still conservative.

The battle began in the Commerce Committee. Dolliver, the Iowa Republican who had been the primary drafter of the president's bill, clashed head on with Aldrich. Aldrich had already accused Dolliver of trying to break up the party with his radical legislation, but the Hepburn-Dolliver bill, which was supported by the president and passed by the House, had powerful strength. Dolliver promised its House supporters that he would get it on the floor of the Senate, substantially unchanged. With help from midwestern Republicans and the Democrats, Dolliver fought for the bill. Its crucial provisions would give the ICC power to replace "unfair" maximum rates, put them immediately into effect, and require properly standardized railroad bookkeeping. These elements, Dolliver explained, were the "three pillars" of proper regulation.

Tempers flared. Aldrich was unable to kill or amend the bill, but he succeeded in two strategems. First, he secured agreement that committee members could offer amendments on the floor of the Senate. Then, though custom dictated that the sponsor of a bill or the committee chairman manage it in the chamber, Aldrich lined up enough Democratic votes to take it away from Dolliver and give it to the Democratic senator from South Carolina, Benjamin Tillman. Thus, if it passed, Tillman and the Democrats would at least share the formal credit. As much as possible Aldrich was trying to arrange that the bill not be presented as a Republican measure, for which members of that party would feel obliged to vote.

When he took the bill out of the hands of its author and ablest exponent, Aldrich gave its management to Tillman, a much less prepared, irascible loner, whose relations with Theodore Roosevelt were bitterly hostile. "Pitchfork" Ben Tillman's vituperative race-baiting had done little to endear him even to many southerners in his own party. When the Senate censured him for striking a fellow senator in the chamber, President Roosevelt had publicly withdrawn an invitation to dinner at the White House. For years, the two had not been speaking terms. Now, Aldrich had maneuvered Tillman into leadership of the president's most important piece of legislation. Dolliver was furious. While Aldrich laughed, Dolliver personally confronted him, saying that it was "a trick too shabby for a gentleman to participate in."[8]

On February 28, 1906, eleven often heated but formally polite weeks of debate began. Although Tillman had been neither well informed nor enthusiastic about the bill, he undertook his responsibility seriously. Commenting that somebody had "come to us unexpectedly and in a great hurry dumped this baby in my arms," he did not propose that "this thing shall be turned into a circus with me as a clown."[9] Once the debate was launched, the senator and the president arrived at a marriage of convenience. They were still not on speaking terms, for Roosevelt was little likely to yield to Tillman's demand for a public apology. However, through a mutual friend, they arrived at a channel of communication and an understanding.

While Dolliver shared the task of defending the bill, Aldrich, along with the ever-ready Joseph Foraker of Ohio, Massachusetts Senator Henry Cabot Lodge, and Pennsylvania's Philander C. Knox, took up the attack. Knox was a distinguished and respected constitutional lawyer. He had been Roosevelt's attorney general, but he genuinely questioned the constitutionality of the proposed law and proved an able new recruit to Aldrich's old guard. The central issue for the conservatives and much of the business community (which had mounted a year-long attack on regulation) was whether the government had the right to tamper with the businessman's control over the price he charged. HR 12987, the Hepburn bill, would give the ICC the right to replace "unfair" maximum rates with prices of its own making. This struck at the heart of business freedom, and to many distinguished lawyers it undermined the fundamental rights of private property.

Apart from Ohio's Foraker, the opponents of the bill were not willing to argue that these rights were absolute. Instead they fell back from arguing over the "rights" of property to its "protection." The best protector was the ponderous, formal, property-oriented judicial system, which had earlier rendered the Interstate Commerce Commission all but meaningless. The opposition pressed its case for a broad, searching, judicial review of commission actions, including suspension of enforcement until the conclusion of litigation and a court rehearing of all the basic evidence upon which a commission decision would be originally made. The actual Senate debate was primarily fought over what kind of a review should be made by the courts. Opponents pointed out with alarm that as it came from the House, the bill had no provision for review at all and, as Knox believed, was therefore probably unconstitutional. Dolliver argued that since review was in the nature of things, of course the courts would have their say. The problem lay among the Democrats, whose votes the bill needed for passage. Some, including Tillman and the vacillating but influential Texas Senator Joe Bailey, wanted a narrow standard of review written in, whereby the courts would only pass on whether the commission had exceeded its powers and had violated the constitutional rights of the railroads. Tillman particularly wanted commission-set rates to be in effect while the courts deliberated, pointing out that cases had taken as much as seventeen years finally to settle.[10]

The fate of the bill was so greatly in doubt that there would not have been much possibility of broadening its scope, even if a significant number of senators had wanted to do so. However, La Follette gave it a try. He had been unsuccessful in getting Roosevelt to support a stronger bill, and now as the debate approached the end of its second month, La Follette rose to make his maiden speech in the Senate. His theme was that the law had to be made stronger to provide for physical evaluation of the railroads and lower rates—and thus prices—for the shippers and consumers.

Soon only a single senator remained in the chamber. "Mr. President," La Follette complained, "I pause in my remarks to say this. I can not be wholly indifferent to the fact that Senators by their absence at this time indicate their want of interest in what I may have to say upon this subject. The public is interested. Unless this important question is rightly settled seats now temporarily vacant may be permanently vacated by those who have the right to occupy them at this time."[11] The galleries applauded, and senators began to drift back into the chamber. La Follette was able to get enough Democratic support to make the Senate take roll call votes on his various amendments, and afterwards he used the recorded votes to campaign against "stand-pat" members (see Document 8). In his 1912 *Autobiography*, he boasted that within a few years, twenty-four of those conservatives were no longer in the Senate.[12] However, all of La Follette's proposals were voted down, and he was to remain contemptuous of Roosevelt for seeking but "half a loaf."

On the other side of the fence, Aldrich's old guard also felt that the president was weak and vacillating, though they did not like the call for an inheritance tax which he combined with his condemnation of journalistic "muck-rakers." Still, some businessmen such as Pennsylvania Railroad President Alexander Cassatt and the retired steel-maker Andrew Carnegie, endorsed regulation. There were continuous strategy conferences in the White House, and the president wrote to his son Kermit that "the political pot is boiling frantically."[13]

The Presidential Compromise

The president's main effort was to find the ground on which he could build sufficient Democratic support to combine with the Republican reformers to get the law passed. This meant that sooner or later he would have to commit himself to a stand on judicial review. In April he finally made his move. To please the Democrats, he endorsed a narrow review position. The months of sparring and delay were yielding to a climax, and both sides rallied their support. When the Democratic minority caucused on April 18, it was Aldrich's tactics and count that seemed correct. The bill needed a minimum of twenty-six Democratic votes—hopefully more. Tillman could muster but twenty-five. The president's "narrow review" strategy had failed.

The details of what happened next are not clear. Defeated in his attempt at coalition with the Democrats on what he hoped were their terms, Roosevelt next swung back to the Republican middle. A new amendment was drafted in the White House. With what historian Blum has called "purposeful obscurity," it provided for judicial review, but in failing to explain what would be the subject of review, left it up to the courts themselves to decide. The amendment was introduced by Iowa Senator William Allison, who had left Aldrich's inner circle to throw his considerable prestige in the Senate on the side of railroad regulation.

Although Allison worked hard on what the White House announced as "the Allison Amendment," he initially disclaimed authorship. Nelson Aldrich's biographer offers a not unpersuasive case for the contention that Aldrich himself drew up the amendment and afterwards contentedly ceased opposition to the bill. The perhaps more judicious historian Blum points out that to leave court review undefined was also a retreat, if not a setback for Aldrich.[14]

However, it is clear that not everybody liked the compromise. Whatever his legislative strategy, the president had publicly abandoned the "narrow review" agreement with Tillman without first telling the proud and contentious South Carolinian. Tillman was furious. He mulled it over for several days before taking what was for him the unusual step of reading a prepared speech to the Senate. In it he told of how he had worked with the president at the latter's request and how, with the help of the attorney general, they had agreed on a position favoring narrow court review. Tillman's incidental comment that the president had named several Republicans as "Senatorial lawyers, who were trying to injure or defeat the bill by ingenious constitutional arguments," sent Henry Cabot Lodge hurrying to a telephone to bring back Roosevelt's reply that this was "a deliberate and unqualified falsehood." The president restated his defense in what his daughter Alice called a "posterity letter" to Lodge. A further Roosevelt letter to Allison, which was read aloud in the Senate, touched off more name-calling.[15]

Although Aldrich shook his head, Tillman bitterly commented that the old guard leader, having almost been unhorsed, had "resumed control of the Republicans."[16] However, the Republican majority was now committed to the railroad bill. Both Roosevelt and Aldrich had compromised. The scope of judicial review was neither narrow nor broad, but rather left to the determination of the Supreme Court, which—in any case—would have had the last word.

Remaining amendments were brought to a vote, and on May 18, HR 12987 passed the Senate. It did so with only the dissent of the unreconciled Foraker and the two Alabama senators. If Aldrich had been there, it was announced, he would have voted for it. Roosevelt and the nation had a railroad law.

The Hepburn Act of 1906 gave an enlarged Interstate Commerce Commission power to act on complaints and replace maximum rates which were not "reasonable and just." Express, sleeping, and all privately owned cars, switching and terminal facilities, and—after a presidential attack on the Standard Oil monopoly—pipeline companies were brought under supervision. Passes were generally forbidden, a triple damage penalty provided for rebating, and a uniform system of accounting required. A "commodities clause" sought to curb unfair competition by preventing interstate railroads from carrying their own products, such as coal, to market. Commission orders were to go into effect in thirty days and were to be binding unless set aside by the courts.

Unanswered in the law was what would happen to commission decisions when they reached the courts. In the 1910 Illinois Central Railroad and the 1912 Union Pacific cases, the Supreme Court resolved this question when it refused to rehear the evidence on which the commission had earlier made its decision.[17] That, said the Court, was the proper fact-determination sphere of the commission. The Court limited its concern to questions of statutory or constitutional authority. Narrow review had prevailed in the Supreme Court. The independent commission as a regulatory instrument was now firmly established. The model was there to be used.

Notes

1. John M. Blum, *The Republican Roosevelt* (Cambridge, Mass.: Harvard University Press, 1952); William H. Harbaugh, *The Life and Times of Theodore Roosevelt* (New York: Farrar, Strauss & Cudahy, 1961, 1963).

2. David J. Rothman, *Politics and Power, The United States Senate, 1869-1901* (Cambridge, Mass.: Harvard University Press, 1966).

3. Roosevelt to Spring Rice, December 27, 1904, in *The Letters of Theodore Roosevelt*, eds. Elting Morison et. al. (Cambridge, Mass.: Harvard University Press, 1951), vol. 4, letter no. 3413, p. 1083.

4. Roosevelt to Trevelyan, March 9, 1905, in *The Letters of Theodore Roosevelt*, letter no. 3438, p. 1133.

5. Theodore Roosevelt, *State Papers*, ed. Hermann Hagedorn (New York: Charles Scribner's Sons, 1926), vol. 15, p. 225.

6. John M. Blum, "Theodore Roosevelt and the Legislative Process: Tariff Revision and Railroad Legislation, 1904-1906," in *The Letters of Theodore Roosevelt*, vol. 4, pp. 1333-42.

7. Roosevelt to Abbott, January 11, 1905, in *The Letters of Theodore Roosevelt*, vol. 4, letter no. 3430, p. 1100.

8. Thomas R. Ross, *Jonathan Prentiss Dolliver* (Iowa City: State Historical Society of Iowa, 1958), p. 206.

9. U.S., Congress, Senate, *Congressional Record,* 59th Cong., 1st sess., 1906, vol. 40, pt. 4, p. 3797; Francis Butler Simkins, *Pitchfork Ben Tillman, South Carolinian* (Baton Rouge: Louisiana State University Press, 1944), pp. 422-24.

10. Simkins, *Ben Tillman,* p. 431.

11. *Congressional Record,* 59th Cong., 1st sess., 1906, vol. 40, pt. 6, p. 5688.

12. *La Follette's Autobiography* (Madison: University of Wisconsin Press, 1960 ed.), p. 179.

13. Roosevelt to Kermit Roosevelt, April 1, 1906, in *The Letters of Theodore Roosevelt,* vol. 5, letter no. 3874, p. 204.

14. John M. Blum, "Theodore Roosevelt and the Hepburn Act: Toward an Orderly System of Control," in *The Letters of Theodore Roosevelt,* vol. 6, pp. 1568-71; Nathaniel Stephenson, *Nelson W. Aldrich* (New York: Charles Scribner's Sons, 1930), pp. 306-15.

15. Simkins, *Ben Tillman,* ch. 28; *Congressional Record,* 59th Cong., 1st sess., 1906, vol. 40, pt. 7, pp. 6774-78, 6787; Roosevelt to Henry Cabot Lodge, May 19, 1906, in *The Letters of Theodore Roosevelt,* vol. 5, letter no. 3917, pp. 273-75.

16. *Congressional Record,* 59th Cong., 1st sess., 1906, vol. 40, pt. 7, p. 6776.

17. *Interstate Commerce Commission v. Illinois Central Railroad Company,* 215 U.S. 452 (1910); *Interstate Commerce Commission v. Union Pacific Railroad Company,* 222 U.S. 541 (1912).

4

The Regulatory Commission Experience

The Commission Pattern

With the passage of the Hepburn Act and its acceptance by the courts, the independent regulatory commission became the primary American way of policing the economy. Combining legislative, executive, and judicial powers, it served as a way of getting around the concerns and qualms which Americans had about each of those branches of government. For those who feared that the courts were too conservative and property-oriented, the executive too potentially dictatorial, and the legislature too self-interested, the very independence of the regulatory commission was appealing. Its powers were delegated by Congress and reviewed by the courts. Its members, selected by the president and approved by the Senate, served for fixed terms, free from the threat of removal and presumably from related pressures. Basically, the commission catered to the general American dislike of government intervention in the economy by divorcing the activities of the commission from the policy control exerted by presidential administrations. The widely held image that the independent regulatory commissions were thus "out of politics" gave them high public standing.

Many kinds of regulation have been undertaken by the regular departments of the government. Agencies from the Food and Drug Administration (FDA) through the Environmental Protection Agency (EPA) have been part of the executive branch. They are authorized by Congress but their direction comes from the administration. The policy-making officials, except those in civil service, hold office at the pleasure of the president. By contrast, the important *independent* regulatory commissions have been the following:

The Interstate Commerce Commission (1887). The ICC regulates rates and practices of railroads, and interstate truck, bus, and oil pipelines.

The Federal Reserve Board (1913). The FED regulates member banks and national bank monetary and credit policies.

The Federal Trade Commission (1914). The FTC regulates monopolistic and unfair business practices, particularly in advertising.

The Federal Power Commission (1930). An outgrowth of the 1920 Water Power Commission, the FPC regulates the transmission and the market behavior of electrical energy and natural gas companies.

The Securities and Exchange Commission (1934). The SEC regulates the stock exchanges and utility holding companies.

The Federal Communications Commission (1934). Supplanting the Federal Radio Commission of 1927, the FCC regulates radio, television, and satellite communication.

The National Labor Relations Board (1935). The NLRB regulates collective bargaining and labor-management practices.

The Federal Maritime Commission (1961). Developing out of the 1916 U.S. Shipping Board, and having gone through various names and roles, the Maritime Commission regulates rates and practices of American ships in international commerce.

The Civil Aeronautics Board (1938). The CAB promotes and regulates the civil air transport industry.

The Tennessee Valley Authority (1935). The TVA is structured like a regulatory commission but it is in reality an ownership and development commission, charged with the decentralized regional socialism and the unified development of the Tennessee Valley.

The Consumer Product Safety Commission (1972). The CPSC sets and enforces safety standards on consumer products.

The Nuclear Regulatory Commission (1975). The NRC retains the control over nonmilitary use of atomic energy first given to the Atomic Energy Commission in 1946. With the termination of the AEC, its research and development responsibility was given to an executive agency, the Energy Research and Development Administration.

For a quarter of a century after the passage of the Hepburn Act of 1906, the independent regulatory commission was the major governmental control over business. During the Progressive Era of the Roosevelt, Taft, and Woodrow Wilson administrations, 1901-1917, the national regulatory principle was applied to banking with the Federal Reserve System and to big business in general with the Federal Trade Commission. This attempted control of transportation, banking, and business, along with the first real use of the Sherman Antitrust law (strengthened somewhat in 1914 by the Clayton Act, which tried more clearly to define "restraint of trade") was aimed at reforming the national business structure. Together with the Pure Food and Drug and Meat Inspection acts of 1906, the income tax provisions of the Underwood-Simmons Tariff reduction law of 1913, and various child labor, industrial accident, and railroad and marine worker protection laws, the national government seemed to be feeling its way toward a regulatory role in important areas of the economy, but still within a capitalist system.

After the end of the emergency controls of World War I and the return of the railroads to private operation, the dominant national political pattern was conservative Republican "normalcy." The Water Power Commission and the Federal Radio Commission were established, but the policy of the Harding-Coolidge-Hoover years was not to regulate or restrain business or to help develop the market power of labor or agriculture. On the whole, business cooperation, combinations, and control of prices were encouraged.

Although in 1911 the Supreme Court ruled against Standard Oil, the Court at the same time in effect amended the antitrust law. The Sherman Act specifically stated that "every combination" which restrained trade was illegal. In the *Standard Oil Company v. U.S.* decision,[1] Chief Justice White interpreted the Sherman Act to mean only "unreasonable" restraints. Market power created by the size of a business was not illegal; the Court would apply the antitrust law only if the market were seized by such wrongful means as espionage, rate discrimination, and local price cutting below costs (which the firm made up in other markets where it had no competition). Thereafter this "rule of reason" tended to govern antitrust cases.

During the 1920s, the Supreme Court reduced the Federal Trade Commission to all but regulatory impotence. In a way reminiscent of what it had done to the Interstate Commerce Commission before the Hepburn Act, the Court refused to accept the FTC's findings of fact, reheard the evidence, and also took over the role of deciding what could be defined as an "unfair practice." In other words, the Supreme Court made itself into a super-Federal Trade Commission, which, on appeal, would do the FTC's job over again, with different conclusions. In addition Congress narrowed the FTC's jurisdiction and Republican presidents appointed new commissioners who opposed regulating business. During these years, the Harding-Coolidge-Hoover Departments of Justice were not very likely to undertake antitrust prosecutions. In fact, Secretary of Commerce Hoover and the Federal Trade Commission encouraged business to develop trade associations, which tended to reduce competition.

With the Stock Market crash of 1929 and the long, bitter depression of the 1930s, the national government became active in the economy to an extent unmatched in peacetime. The big problem was to revive what had become a low production, employment, and purchasing power economy. The New Deal tried many methods on an often hit-or-miss experimental basis. It initially kept the Sherman antitrust law on the shelf and turned the trade associations of the 1920s into government enforced, price and practice fixing cartels under the National Industrial Recovery Act (NIRA). When the Supreme Court declared this to be an unconstitutional delegation of power and use of the commerce clause,[2] Franklin Roosevelt turned to the antitrust laws to stimulate competition and production.

The federal government also engaged in large-scale spending on relief and on public projects. It sought to limit agricultural production and bought up surpluses in an effort to increase farm income. Among other governmental thrusts into the economy, the government tried to protect natural resources, prevent erosion, and generally to develop the whole region through which the flood-prone Tennessee River flowed. In a mixture of economic and social goals, the government supported union organization, wage and hour standards, mortgage relief, the protection of individual bank deposits, and care of the elderly and dependent. All of this meant new ways to handle old institutions and problems, and pioneering attempts to deal with new areas.

Usually New Deal programs were undertaken by a new government agency under presidential policy direction. Sometimes this meant the use of the independent regulatory commission. Often it meant a combination of executive and independent regulatory efforts, which was to become standard in the emerging mixed capitalism of America in the twentieth century. The Federal Reserve Board, an independent regulatory commission, was strengthened, but shared supervision of banks and money supply with the administrative agencies of the Federal Deposit Insurance Corporation (FDIC) and the Comptroller of the Currency. The Securities Exchange Commission (SEC) was set up to regulate the stock markets and was later given supervision of the structure of utility holding companies. The National Labor Relations Board (NLRB) was created to supervise the labor-management relations involved with the growth of unions and collective bargaining. A new kind of independent regulatory commission, the Tennessee Valley Authority, or TVA, was set up to build dams, prevent floods, sell power, improve transportation, and undertake the planned development of the whole region. Commissions were strengthened, revised, or created, to work with the radio, shipping, power, trucking, and aviation industries.

After World War II, the government remained a major force in the market and the economy. The Employment Act of 1946 was a formal assumption by the government of responsibility to maintain production and employment at suitable national levels. The government continued to use its monetary, tax, and spending policies to achieve this goal, in the Republican administrations of Eisenhower, Nixon, and Ford, as well as in the Democratic administrations of Truman, Kennedy, and Johnson. Republicans initiated a national highway building program, used temporary peacetime antiinflation wage and price controls; Richard Nixon announced that he was a follower of John Maynard Keynes. Two new independent regulatory commissions were created: in 1946, the Atomic Energy Commission was set up to handle the peaceful uses of atomic energy, and in 1972 growing consumer concern produced the Consumer Product Safety Commission.

Historically, then, what has been the role of the independent regulatory commission? At the beginning of the century, the commission seemed destined to be the prime instrument for government intervention in the economy. What the "automatic" mechanism of the market could not do, the "minimum interference" instrument of the independent regulatory commission would. The American belief in an enterpriser, or market society, more or less came to include the role of a "fourth branch" of government which would be independent, and thus not "political." This view remains a basic American way of regulation. While other forms of direct government intervention are seen as somehow extraordinary and temporary, the independent regulatory commission is accepted as a part of the order of things, particularly in the areas of transportation, power, the stock market, collective bargaining, communication, and in such special fields as the TVA and atomic power. Its concerns have been primarily those of business prices, practices, and advertising.

Shortcomings or Failure?

However, the history of twentieth-century America has been one of explosive social and technological development, war, inflation, depression and crisis. As Brandeis University President Marver Bernstein has observed, economic problems facing the country have gone "far beyond the limited scope of economic regulation."[3] The government has acted deeply in the economy to stimulate, guide, and particularly in time of war, to control it. Bigness in industry and government have been characteristic of the world's leading economy. The regulatory commission process, operating on a slow, case-by-case, juridical basis, has declined in importance, and criticism of the regulatory commission approach has mounted (*Alternatives 4 and 5:* see Document 15).

There have been two major complaints about this "fourth branch" of government. The basic function of the independent regulatory commission has been to protect the business man and consumer from monopoly or big business abuse. However, the case-by-case approach of most commissions makes it impossible for them to offer constructive guidance for the future course of the industries they oversee. The second complaint is that the regulatory commissions have become not only the captives of their own complex legal procedures, but also of the industries that they are supposed to regulate.

At the very least, the commissions have tried to work in harmony with their industries. Over time, the men appointed as commissioners tend to come from those industries, particularly from their legal departments. This has increased the tendency of commissions to see themselves as "courts" settling the specific issues that rise out of the conduct of business, rather than guiding or battling with their industries. Commissioners are generally not well known and are not selected for their political strength or new ideas. The "idea men" in American society stay in business or the professions, run for office, or go into the upper levels of national administrations. Although there is a rapid turnover on the commissions, they have not been stepping stones upward in politics. The defeated former office holder, not the ambitious, rising one, goes to the commission. A commissioner who draws particular attention to himself by censuring the practices of the industry he is to regulate is usually not reappointed. Such was the experience of Federal Power Commissioner Leland Olds, who tried to keep down natural gas prices in the 1940s, and of Newton Minow, John Kennedy's Federal Communications Commission chairman, who was bold enough to attack the "educational wastelands" of television. Marver Bernstein, the commission authority, has graphically described what typically happens: "Politically isolated, lacking a firm basis of public support, lethargic in attitude and approach, bowed down by precedent and backlogs, unsupported in its demands for more staff and money, the commission finally becomes a captive of the regulated groups."[4] It is not a matter of having been purchased, but rather one of maintaining the status quo and of seeing things from the industry's point of view. The customer, consumer, commuter, would-be trucker, and unscheduled airline are outsiders.

Originally Congress expected commissions to work for the general public interest and to provide Congress with the facts and advice—the expert knowledge—it needed to make future policy. However, living in a world of lawyers, courts, and industry pressure, understaffed, and static in their procedures, the commissions have rarely provided this expertise or national planning guidance.

Increasingly since the 1930s, such policy guidance has seemed necessary. Fron Franklin Roosevelt onward, presidents have sought to bring the independent regulatory commissions under the control of their administrations. They have suggested changes ranging from revitalization to abolition, and they have regularly asked that the commissions report to or work with executive agencies.

However, the commissions were created to be separate and have remained that way. Even long-time ICC Commissioner Joseph B. Eastman, perhaps the ablest of the independent regulators, was distressed by Franklin Roosevelt's attempt to draw the ICC into his administration. When FDR sought to fire the extremely conservative, Coolidge-appointed chairman of the Federal Trade Commission, the Supreme Court overruled the president.[5]

Since 1937, five major governmental studies, including President Truman's Hoover Commission, John Kennedy's Landis Report, and the study by Roy Ash, who became Richard Nixon's head of the Office of Management and Budget, have criticized the regulatory commissions for their weakness and ineffectiveness. In the late 1960s and 1970s, consumer advocate Ralph Nader was scathing in his attacks on commission failure. While President Ford, who wanted less government in business, sharply attacked governmental regulation for forcing up costs and prices, Congress moved toward establishing a new consumer representative who would speak for the public before the regulatory commissions.

Notes

1. *Standard Oil Company v. United States*, 221 U.S.1 (1911).

2. *Panama Refining Company v. Ryan*, 293 U.S. 388 (1935); *Schecter v. United States*, 295 U.S. 495 (1935).

3. Marver Bernstein, *Regulating Business by Independent Commission* (Princeton: Princeton University Press, 1955), p. 90.

4. Marver Bernstein, "Independent Regulatory Agencies: A Perspective on Their Reform," *The Annals of the American Academy of Political and Social Science*, vol. 400 (March, 1972), pp. 14-26.

5. *Humphrey's Executor v. United States*, 295 U.S. 602 (1935).

5

Railroads:
The Enduring
Problem

The Sick Railroads

By the 1970s, the Interstate Commerce Commission, America's first national independent regulatory commission, was ninety years old. Seventy years had passed since the Hepburn Act of 1906 had strengthened it and made it a model for American regulatory capitalism. By the 1970s, the railroads, still vital to the national economy, were in a state of collapse. A semi-nationalization of intercity passenger traffic was proving ineffective. The two great trunk lines of the East, the New York Central and the Pennsylvania, had been combined into the giant Penn Central system, mismanaged, looted, and finally left in bankruptcy and threatened liquidation. While railroads in other parts of the country were solvent, those of the Northeast and Midwest were in serious straits. It seemed likely that the nation would have to celebrate its bicentennial years by a governmental reorganization and subsidization of the northeast lines and a probable quasi-nationalization of their trackbeds. This final chapter will look at what happened to the railroads after the passage of the Hepburn Act, briefly examining the role which the Hepburn's solution, the independent regulatory commission, has played in the developing railroad crisis of the twentieth century.

In the years after the newly strengthened ICC emerged from the Hepburn Act, Congress continued to expand its powers and role. The act gave the commission power only to replace "unreasonable and unjust" maximum rates after they had gone into effect. In 1910, the Mann-Elkins Act extended control to newly proposed rates and the right to act without waiting for a shipper's complaint. Restrictions against different charges for long and short hauls were strengthened. Jurisdiction over all forms of railroad carriers and pipelines was extended to telegraph, telephone, and cable systems. A special Commerce Court, favored by President Taft, was established to hear appeals from ICC orders. When the court set itself strongly in opposition to the commission, Congress killed it, over the president's veto. The Panama Canal Act added supervision over relations between railroads and water carriers. The Valuation Act of 1913 finally gave the commission authority to meet Senator La Follette's desire for valuation as a base for rate determination. In 1914, the antitrust law was strengthened by an amendment known as the Clayton Act, which tried to bolster competition by prohibiting railroads from buying up their competitors.

Should it be assumed that by the second decade of the century the nation had finally achieved a sound, prosperous railroad system, guided by a strong and able independent regulatory commission? The answer is neither clear nor particularly favorable. The ICC did have supervisory control over rates, discriminatory practices, and some areas of safety. Its role was to oversee how the railroads treated passengers and shippers. This was primarily a rate and service, sometimes called a "negative" regulation. Its goals were the achievement of competition and nondiscrimination. It had no control over railroad capitalization, finances, and labor relations. It was not charged or concerned with the long-range goals of a national railroad system. There were no premonitions yet of a world in which the automobile, bus, truck, and airplane might challenge the railroads, or even that pipelines and barges might cut substantially into railroad revenues.

Wages, taxes, and general costs were going up, but the ICC turned down railroad requests for substantial rate increases. Despite expanding freight and passenger traffic, the operating ratio for the railroads (the ratio between operating costs and revenue) moved up to over seventy percent.[1] More and more the railroads raised capital by fixed, interest-paying borrowing, rather than by selling stock. Railroad men, seconded by the historian Albro Martin, lamented the inability of the railroads to obtain sufficient cash flow from the market and have blamed it on public hostility and the ICC.[2]

However, it is difficult to place major fault on the public, the regulators, or Theodore Roosevelt for the long-range financial troubles of the railroads. The railroads did face a money squeeze, but the speculative mania that produced the so-called rich man's panic of 1907 originated in Wall Street, not in the White House or in legislative or commission chambers. The railroads were overcapitalized and the Harrimans, Goulds, and their successors seemed always ready for new, costly, manipulative ventures.

The serious complaint made by current railroad historians, freed from the Populist-Progressive-New Deal hostility toward big business, is that the attempt to maintain a regulated competitive system could only damage the railroads. Their argument is that railroad management would have created order if it had not been prevented from doing so: the crucial error was that Congress prohibited pooling when first setting up the ICC in 1887. In their view, the "sensible" path of voluntary cooperation among the railroads was rejected in favor of the more restrictive approach of the Interstate Commerce and Sherman acts.[3] From that point, Albro Martin comments, "it was all downhill."[4] When the Hepburn Act made the ICC an effective force some twenty years later, they argue, it used its power to prevent the railroads from managing their rates and operations with sufficient flexibility to adjust to larger economic changes.

This is an important issue. Since World War I, there has been widespread agreement that a sound national railway system needed to be guided into existence. Until the 1970s, public opinion, the Congress, the ICC, and the railroads were not ready to work out a cooperative path. The judicious historian John Stover, writing about the failure of voluntary cooperation among the railroads during World War I, noted that even in this moment of national crisis "a highly competitive individualism continued to exist."[5] With the exception of World War II, this was to be true through the hard years of the depression and up to the present. Even by the early 1970s, the severity of the problem had not particularly inclined the railroads to make AMTRAK (a contraction of American Track), the government's national passenger system, a success. The railroads have undertaken marvels of innovation and technology, but there have always been major cases of misbehavior—such as J.P. Morgan's manipulation of the Boston & Maine, the Moore brothers' handling of the Rock Island, the twisted financial history of the Van Sweringens' pyramided Allegheny Corporation, and the management of the Penn Central—to raise serious questions about free market solutions to the management of American railroads (*Alternative 2*: see Documents 16 and 17).

In 1916, the American railroad system reached its greatest extension when it totaled some 254,000 miles. Sometime around that year, more people had come to live in cities than in small towns and in the countryside. It was also the tenth anniversary of the Hepburn Act. In 1916, three federal laws were passed which can be taken to symbolize the future problems of the railroads as America's dominant, privately-owned, profit-making transportation system. These were the Adamson Act, which set an eight-hour day for railroad labor, the Federal Highway Act, providing matching funds for state highway building, and the provision in the Army Appropriation Act giving the government authority to take over the railroads. During the next fifty years, increasing labor costs and antiquated work rules, and competition from cars, trucks, and airplanes using government subsidized roads and airports, were to become major factors in the decline of the railroads. In the 1970s a quasi-government ownership of the railroads was to be the attempted solution.

The Adamson Act, passed in 1916 and upheld by the Supreme Court the following year,[6] cut the work day from ten to eight hours, with no loss of pay. After Woodrow Wilson had been unsuccessful in getting the railroad presidents to accept the eight-hour day, he had turned to Congress for legislation to prevent a major strike which would have crippled the country's booming war-supply economy.

The railroad take-over provision had originally been written into the Army Appropriation Act for possible use in a conflict with Mexico, but President Wilson was soon to have other need for it. With the nation at war with Germany the following year, voluntary coordination of transportation did not work. Each railroad competitively sought the largest possible share of the wartime traffic, ticketed its freight as priority, and shipped its cars off to the Eastern ports. By the late fall of 1917, almost two hundred thousand freight cars were jammed up on the East Coast. There was a dangerous shortage of cars elsewhere and a threatened coal famine in ice-bound New England.

On the day after Christmas, the president took possession of the railroads. Within months, under the direction of the able secretary of the treasury, William Gibbs McAdoo, the tangle was straightened out. Cars were moved over the shortest routes, unloaded, and sent back again. Passenger service was unified, priorities applied, luxury service terminated, new engines and rolling stock ordered, operations standardized, and rails and roads brought into shape. It was an example of outstanding administrative skill and of the benefits of the planned, unified operation of the national rail system in a time of emergency.

The costs of a government-run rail system are open to greater controversy. The operating United States Railroad Administration raised wages and to a lesser degree, rates. Through its various expenditures to bring the railroads into shape, it ended up in the red, although the final deficit included payment of an estimated 8½ percent profit to the companies, calculated from their averages over the preceding three years. The government had performed well in untangling a major snarl and getting the war transportation job done, but whether government operation was as economical as capitalist control was another issue. Much of the question of evaluation of the government's role revolves around whether it was too generous to labor or too open to labor pressures—and operating ratios were very high.

"Guided Capitalism"

After the war, the big railroad unions, the Brotherhoods, wanted the government to keep the railroads. Their proposal, named for their lawyer, was called the Plum Plan. However, on March 1, 1920, the railroads were given back to their owners, after twenty-six months of government control. Just before the return, Congress had passed the Esch-Cummins Act of 1920. For the first time the ICC was given a concrete standard for measuring an adequate rate of return for the railroads. This standard was set at 5½ percent. If profits were over 6 percent, half of the surplus would be held by the railroad to cover any future bad year, and half would be used by the ICC to help weaker companies. The power of the ICC was extended to setting minimum rates and supervision of railroad financial policies, including new stock issues, mergers, and consolidations. The prohibition of pooling, established in the original law of 1887, was reversed.

The war experience and railroad needs, had brought about a fundamental change in regulatory outlook. Previously the goals had been restrictive; the commission had sought to control rates and discrimination. Now it was charged with "fostering" a sound, adequate national railroad system. Toward that end, the commission for the first time was directed to prepare a plan for combining the existing railroads into a limited number of efficient and profitable, though competing, systems.

At least for the next half-century—until the mid-1970s—the commission was not able either to produce such a system or to devise a plan for one. With the exception of long-time Commissioner Joseph B. Eastman, there was little enthusiasm for it on the commission itself. The railroads, despite often diastrous financial conditions, were hostile. It was not that the railroads were opposed to consolidation on their own terms, however. Over Eastman's protests, the commission permitted the Van Sweringen brothers to build a "watered" railroad empire in the Midwest, and the Pennsylvania, the New York Central, and the Baltimore & Ohio spent hundreds of millions of dollars during the "big bull market" of the late 1920s and into the first years of the depression, buying stock in smaller roads.

The guided capitalism of the independent regulatory commission was a failure. While shippers and consumers generally benefited from rate and discrimination control, a sound transportation system did not emerge. A vigorous antiunion campaign helped force down railroad wages. The recapture provisions were circumvented, and unified planning was not seriously undertaken. As before, market strength still governed. The authors of a recent text on "Government and the Economy" summed up the experience of the 1920s, writing that:

> "Railway security issues were supervised, but financial control groups discovered legal and other subterfuges which rendered them largely immune from ICC control. Management continued to be dependent on the control groups; consolidations were determined, not by the ICC or by the needs of the weak railroads, but by the stronger roads and their affiliated investment bankers. The effects of extravagant expenditures for stock purchases and wide distribution of dubious holding-company securities were shortly to prove disastrous for many small investors."[7]

Even during the desperate days of the Great Depression of the 1930s, no group—the railroads, the ICC, the Congress, or the executive branch—worked forcefully for a unified transportation policy. And the depression was disastrous for the railroads. Operating revenues fell to less than half. Despite wage cuts, firings, declining maintenance, and government loans, almost a third of the railroads went into receivership.[8] Most of the others were close to it. In 1932, for example, almost three-quarters of the major, or class I, railroads failed to earn enough to pay their fixed charges. Freight traffic had collapsed along with the economy, and credit and investment funds were not available.

In addition to providing loans, the federal government extended the regulation of railroad finances and again halfheartedly tried to seek a plan for a national railroad system. With new Bankruptcy and Emergency Transportation acts in 1933, the ICC now gained supervision of railroad holding companies and of bankruptcies. The debt structure of bankrupt railroads was revised. Capitalization was reduced, with much of the bonded debt shifted to stocks. This had the dual effect of diminishing railroad indebtedness and rendering investors much less enthusiastic about future railroad ventures.

Under the Emergency Transportation Act, Joseph B. Eastman became Federal Coordinator of Transportation, but he could not get the railroads to work out plans for a unified system and was not willing to push for either public ownership or a forced consolidation of the roads. Despite the efforts of Montana Senator Burton K. Wheeler, and after long Commerce Committee hearings, public and congressional sentiment generally opposed basic changes. Jurisdiction over trucking and interstate water carriers was given the ICC by the 1935 Motor Carrier and the 1940 Transportation acts. However, many exceptions were made to this grant of authority, and air travel was placed under its own independent regulator, the Civil Aeronautics Board.

World War II was a prosperous time for the American economy and the railroads. Unlike conditions during World War I when shipments piled up at the East Coast ports, battle fronts in the Atlantic and the Pacific meant a better two-way utilization of the rails. Except for a month-long strike, the industry avoided governmental takeover by cooperation with federal transportation directors, the durable Eastman, now head of the Office of Defense Transportation, and former Burlington Railroad President Ralph Budd, who headed the Office of Emergency Management. The railroads performed well, moved the troops and supplies, made money, and paid off a further portion of their debts.

However, after the wartime interruption, the decline of the railroads began again. Basic shifts in modes of transportation, governmental policies and favoritism, natural and economic hardships, and the behavior of the railroads themselves, played parts. Most important was the maturation of alternate forms of passenger and freight transportation. When the Hepburn Act was passed in 1906, the railroads had close to a monopoly. Only water and pipeline carriage gave them any competition. After World War II the motor car, truck, bus, pipeline, inland water carrier, and airplane came of age. The passengers and the railroads had all but deserted each other. People traveled by plane, car, or bus. At the end of the 1960s, the railroads carried less than ten percent of the intercity travel. In the movement of freight, measured by ton miles,[9] the ICC reported[10] that the 1972 percentages were as follows:

Railroads	37.77
Motor vehicles	22.63
Inland waterways, including the Great Lakes	16.31
Pipelines (oil)	23.11
Airways	.18

On the whole, the railroad passenger business had long been a money loser. For short haul freight, and for less than carload lots, trucks were better. For long hauls of carload lots, the railroads, which pulled rather than carried the freight, had lower costs and greater operating efficiency. They needed less horsepower per ton mile than the trucks and used less fuel.[11]

For the past half-century, government policy has both restricted the railroads and aided their competitors. The railroads have had to maintain and pay taxes on their rail lines, yards, and terminals, but local, state, and national governments have provided roads and airports for the use of their competitors. By the 1970s, a three and one-half million mile road and highway network was being topped off by a forty-thousand mile interstate superhighway system.[12]

As a result of various exemptions written into the regulatory acts, much of the truck and waterway activity was free of federal supervision. Meanwhile the railroads suffered from two disadvantageous kinds of regulation. One was the extent and slowness of commission decision-making. The other was a principle established in the Transportation Act of 1940 and not reversed until the act was revised in 1950, which prevented the railroads from lowering their rates to compete with trucks and water carriers. The original purpose had been to try to develop and protect each of the kinds of transportation, but in effect it served mainly to handicap the hard beset railroads.

A further damaging situation for the railroads was caused by outdated and costly work rules for labor. If communities and the ICC found it difficult to permit the railroads to change rates or abandon little-used routes and stations, union power made it all but impossible to eliminate expensive "feather-bedding" practices. Such practices as using new crews every 100 to 150 miles and the continued employment of unnecessary firemen placed costly burdens on already staggering railroad finances. The railroad unions were generally able to protect jobs in a declining industry at the cost of pushing it precariously toward the wall. From the 1930s onward to the governmental consolidation of the bankrupt northeastern railroads in the 1970s, strikes and government intercession prevented changes in work rules or required the railroads to assume costly pension systems for laid-off trainmen.

As with all enterprise, the railroads had to face the burdens of economic change, natural catastrophe, and the ups and downs of the economy. In the past, the sustaining freight traffic of the railroads had benefited from growth in the heavy manufacturing sector of the economy, whose bulk products the railroads were best fitted to carry. As growth in what is sometimes called a "postindustrial America" shifted to light manufacturing and service industries, the railroads no longer automatically benefited from economic expansion.

Storm and flood damage, such as that brought by Hurricane Agnes which forced the Erie Lackawana into bankruptcy in 1972, cut income and damaged already disintegrating roadbeds. Strikes in the steel, motor car, and coal industries, and on the railroads themselves, helped make the sick industry sicker. When the inflation of the early 1970s combined with an economic downturn, the roads were further caught in a credit and operating cash squeeze that increasingly forced many of them toward bankruptcy.

Finally, somewhere amid the arguments of their detractors and defenders, lies the contribution which the railroads themselves made to their own troubles. To their credit, they spent billions of dollars on new equipment and new efforts. They poured money into diesels and electrification, high-speed Metro-liners between Washington and New York, all aluminium trains, vista domes, new types of freight cars, coal-carrying unit trains whose cars were never uncoupled or turned around, and electronic and computerized control systems.

Nevertheless having generally written off passenger travel as a losing proposition, the railroads seemed intent on making it as uncomfortable as possible. Perhaps the great monarchs of an era of rails—the Santa Fe *Super Chief*, the Burlington *Zephyr*, the New York Central *Twentieth Century Limited*, the Pennsylvania *Broadway Limited*, and the Erie Lackawanna *Phoebe Snow*—had to go. At the same time, with more than passing justification, critics charged that the railroads too often tried to run their potentially profitable freight business along rigid, traditional lines, scorning the salesmanship, innovativeness, and service consciousness that could utilize natural railroad efficiencies and advantages. And, as always, the railroads maneuvered among themselves to gain advantage for their own roads, rather than cooperating in sharing facilities and planning an overall sound consolidated system or systems.

Disaster in the 1970s

Disaster struck in the 1970s. It was so perilous to the railroads and to the whole American economy that the nation was obliged to turn a transportation corner in order to work on survival. On June 21, 1970, the giant of the American railroads, the $4.5 billion Penn Central Railroad went bankrupt. It had been put together only a little more than two years before, after a decade of delicate negotiation. In the beginning, it represented a latter-day fulfillment of the dream that J.P. Morgan may have held on that day in 1885 when he sequestered the presidents of the battling New York Central and Pennsylvania Railroads aboard his yacht, *Corsair*, which steamed up and down the Hudson until they agreed to cooperate. Now the nation's greatest railroad conglomerate had been created, with its real estate, hotels, basketball and ice hockey teams, and twenty thousand miles of track in the industrial heartland of America.

The officials of the new Penn Central fought among themselves in merger, as they had in independent operation. Below them, no one knew what was going on, and there was chaos. Labor costs remained high. Passenger service was miserable and lost money. More money went out in dividends and in large nonrailroad investments, including an executive jet rental service that also supplied call girls, and a secret bank account in the little European country of Liechtenstein. Large bond issues were maturing and short-term commercial paper was due. The Defense Department refused to guarantee a major, long-term loan, and the flow of cash was not sufficient to handle day-to-day expenses. Despite multibillion dollar assets, Penn Central went bankrupt. Its losses during its second and final year of private operation were close to two hundred million dollars (see Document 18).

The government had not kept the Penn Central out of bankruptcy, but to let the trains stop running was something else. Without the Penn Central, General Motors avowed, the production of automobiles would come to a swift halt. So would all of the northeastern United States, the majority leader of the House of Representatives stated. But what could be done to "save" the northeastern railroads?

According to the ICC, "the last generally good year for rail operations" had been 1966.[13] The western and southern railroads were generally in the black and in the East, the two coalfield lines, the Norfolk & Western and the enlarged Chesapeake & Ohio, or "Chessie," were doing well. However, by 1975, seven northeastern and midwestern roads had joined the Penn Central in bankruptcy and more of the grain-hauling "granger" roads were in trouble.

Along with the Penn Central, the bankrupt roads were the Erie Lackawanna, the Reading, the Lehigh Valley, the Central of New Jersey, the Lehigh & Hudson, the Ann Arbor, and the Rock Island.

For the railroad industry as a whole, the return on invested capital seldom ventured as high as three percent in recent years and even profitable railroads were below the market level. As *Business Week* summed it up: "Most companies are not earning enough money to renew themselves or build for future traffic. They cannot generate enough funds internally, cannot attract loans, and they certainly cannot attract equity [investors' money through new stock issues]." [14]

In the 1970s, the government began to take a central place in the railroad picture. It acted in three ways. First, in the tradition of the depression era Reconstruction Finance Corporation, it provided grants and loan guarantees to keep the bankrupt Penn Central operating. Second, while states such as New York and Pennsylvania helped keep commuter railroad services going, the national government assumed responsibility for a pared-down intercity passenger system, which it named AMTRAK. Third, by mid-decade, the government was moving toward creating what the New York *Times* called "private enterprise socialism" [15] with the bankrupt Northeast and Midwest freight carriers.

On the first of May, 1971, the newly established National Railroad Passenger Corporation, better known as AMTRAK, began to run its trains. Created by Congress as an alternative to the almost complete disappearance of long-haul intercity railroad passenger travel, it was to run some 186 trains over a cut-down national network. With only forty million dollars outright plus loans and loan guarantees of three hundred million more for roadbed repair, equipment, and running expenses, AMTRAK was meant to be self-supporting by the time the money ran out. This did not happen. The system was critically underfunded, existing tracks and roadbeds were in such prohibitively bad condition that trains—often themselves old and poorly maintained—seldom arrived on time. To make matters worse, the railroads, whom AMTRAK paid to run its trains, showed all too little concern about AMTRAK succeeding. Although passenger use increased, AMTRAK continued to depend on further congressional funding for solvency.

The condition of the industry worsened, particularly in the Northeast. Although use and revenues increased, costs went up more rapidly. Funds were not available to maintain and upgrade roadbeds and equipment; cars slowed over unsafe track; and a tightened money market and a declining national economy cut the roads off from sufficient operating income. Faced with spreading railroad bankruptcy in the crucial industrial areas of the East, the nation edged toward a new giant step.

In 1973, Congress created a U.S. Railway Association (USRA) to come up with a plan for the Penn Central and the other bankrupt northeastern roads. In July of 1975, the plan went before Congress, which had sixty days to accept, change, or reject it. As the time approached, the plight of the industry became more grave and alternatives fewer. The plan called for the creation of two new corporations. Consolidated Facilities, or CONFAC, was to rehabilitate and maintain the track system in seventeen northeastern and midwestern states. Unless the states would take over an important share of the cost, some five thousand seven hundred miles of lesser used track would be abandoned. The second corporation, Consolidated Railroads, or CONRAIL, would run the freight plus a special high-speed passenger corridor from Boston to Washington, D.C. Critical estimates were that the government would be spending at least ten billion dollars over a fifteen year period. According to the proposed law, at least as long as it was putting up the money, the national government would appoint the directors of the two corporations. While there was some discussion of outright governmental ownership, it seemed unlikely that the Congress would go that far. The plan still talked of "competition" between various railroad lines in and out of CONFAC and CONRAIL and much of the business community joined President Ford in calling for less rather than more government regulation. (*Alternative 4:* see Document 19).

The Alternatives: Seventy Years After

Nearly ninety years of federal railroad regulation had not produced a sound railroad system. While far from having the transportation monopoly they had in 1887, when the ICC was created, and 1906, when the Hepburn Act was passed, the railroads were still crucial. At the beginning of the century, as the United States emerged as the world's leading industrial power, there had seemed to be six general alternatives for insuring a healthy system. Antitrust laws (*Alternative 1*) survive today and experience periods of important revival. However they have served more as a threat against improper behavior than as a basic operating principle. While a degree of competition would likely remain among the railroads, the path ahead would be one of growing consolidation.

Looking at the failures of regulation to provide economic health, there have been those who felt that the government should withdraw from the field or minimize its activites (*Alternative 2*). However, the history of the twentieth century strongly indicated that this was not seriously possible. The railroad managers who have been most critical of regulation have not been able to either consolidate or to go it on their own. For the plight of the northeastern railroads, the market had offered no solutions.

The further development of a national and world economy, and the extent of railroad problems in the twentieth century, have made basic regulation by the individual states (*Alternative 3*) seem even less possible than it did in 1906.

The path chosen during the Progressive Era was the independent regulatory commission, and so the ICC was strengthened by the Hepburn Act of 1906. Extended by additional legislation (*Alternative 6*), it has been used as a model in the fields of transportation, energy, and big business. As the problems and needs of the economy became more complex, the focus shifted from the regulation of rates and discrimination to the maintenance of a sound national transportation system.

It has often been charged that the ICC developed a community of outlook and values with the industry it regulated, although the shippers—perhaps the prime interest group behind the ICC and Hepburn laws—may well have had reason to be satisfied on the issues of rates and discriminations. However, there seems to be general agreement that the slowness of commission decision-making has been an important factor in creating the financial problems faced by the railroads. While an industry such as steel, even when operating at a high level of demand and profit, can further raise its prices almost at will, the railroads, beset by low rates, woefully inadequate profits and operating funds, have found that rate increases also come slowly and inadequately. In the turned corner of the railroad world of the 1970s, the Interstate Commerce Commission has few admirers.

Over the years, the powers of the commission were extended (*Alternative 4*). By the advent of the depression, the ICC had gained the extended rate-setting, physical evaluation, and financial regulation control that Robert La Follette fought for during the early 1900s. With the national passenger service AMTRAK and the proposed governmental consolidation of the northeast railroads, a form of Senator Francis Newland's program for national incorporation, consolidation, and regulation, seemed to be coming to life. Those who saw the national government as more than a passive, or negative, regulatory force, had most correctly predicted the future. Perhaps in the 1970s—in a world more complex than either had imagined—there were growing elements of La Follette's concern about the consumer and Newland's press for a more rationalized economy. However, the mixed-economy solution for the American rail system, as has been the habit of the nation, defied a close fit into any one clear pattern.

Governmental ownership (*Alternative 5*) seemed neither unreasonable nor likely in the 1970s. Practically every major industrial country had a better functioning railroad system than the United States. Americans talked with envy of super trains such as the Japanese "bullet-train" that zipped passengers past Mount Fuji in comfort at more than a hundred miles an hour and arrived at its destination on time. However while the Swiss system made a profit, other nationalized railroads had to be subsidized, and there were problems. The difficulties of the American railroads seemed greater in comparison and the American government was increasingly becoming involved in their financing and operation. There were those who questioned why a nation that was willing to spend twenty-five billion dollars to place a man on the moon should be so reluctant about spending lesser sums to shape up and maintain a necessary railroad system.

Consistently through the twentieth century, a few voices within the political center called for nationally owned railroads. In the mid-1970s, as the passenger and northeastern rail systems came increasingly under governmental control, it was possible to talk about nationalization without being subjected to heated denunciation. Even so, perhaps Senate Commerce Committee

Chairman Vance Hartke, was correct when he commented that the American people were not ready for this alternative. They were closer to it than they had ever been before, but, as the New York *Times* phrased it, a "private-enterprise socialism" which was "distinct from anything ever envisaged by either Adam Smith or Karl Marx" seemed what they were eventually going to try.[16] After one hundred years "the whole thing" as the Illinois "granger" legislator had called the railroad problem, still remained far from settled.

Notes

1. John Stover, *The Life and Decline of the American Railroad* (New York: Oxford University Press, 1970), p. 117.

2. Albro Martin, *Enterprise Denied* (New York: Columbia University Press, 1971).

3. Ibid.; K. Austin Kerr, *American Railroad Politics, 1914-1920* (Pittsburgh: University of Pittsburgh Press, 1968).

4. Albro Martin, "The Troubled Subject of Railroad Regulation in the Gilded Age-A Reappraisal," *The Journal of American History*, vol. 61 (September, 1974), p. 352.

5. Stover, *The Life and Decline of the American Railroad*, p. 164.

6. *Wilson v. New*, 243 U.S. 332 (1917).

7. Merle Fainsod, Lincoln Gordon, and Joseph C. Palamountain, *Government and the American Economy* (New York: W.W. Norton, 1959), p. 277.

8. When a railroad was unable to meet its debts, a court often appointed a receiver to supervise the railroad and to protect its assets while the court sought to reorganize it and scale down its debts to prevent bankruptcy and liquidation.

9. A ton mile is the number of tons multiplied by the distance or number of miles, they were carried.

10. Interstate Commerce Commission, *87th Annual Report to Congress* (Washington, D.C.: Government Printing Office, 1972), p. 7.

11. Stover, *The Life and Decline of the American Railroad*, pp. 238-39.

12. See Richard O. Davies, *The Age of Asphalt* (Philadelphia: J.B. Lippincott Co., 1975).

13. Interstate Commerce Commission, *86th Annual Report to Congress* (Washington, D.C.: Government Printing Office, 1972), p. 7.

14. "How to lose money in a rising market," *Business Week*, September 14, 1974, p. 1960.

15. A.H. Raskin, "The Dirty Word on U.S. Railroads: Nationalize," New York *Times Weekly Review*, March 2, 1972, p. 2.

16. Ibid.

part two

Documents of the Decision

1

The Growing Consolidation of Railroad Control

In its authoritative and widely quoted 1902 report, the Industrial Commission provided information on the growing concentration of control, or what it called "community of interest," in the hands of a few financial groups.

Document†
FINAL REPORT OF THE INDUSTRIAL COMMISSION
Community of interest among railroads in the United States

SUMMARY

Groups	Mileage
Vanderbilt	19,517
Morgan	19,073
Harriman	20,245
Pennsylvania	18,220
Gould	16,074
Hill	10,373
Belmont	4,430
Belmont-Morgan	532
	108,464
Independent	37,977

CHARACTERISTICS AND OBJECTS OF RECENT CONSOLIDATIONS

The consolidations of the last two years not only contrast strongly in magnitude with those of earlier years; they are at the same time essentially different in character. The purpose of the earlier combinations was in the main to secure business by extension of lines and feeders to strategic points. As has been properly said by Professor Hull: "They were primarily administered not geographically; each aimed to handle its own traffic and to secure a strong position. A strong position was useful in adjusting a pool with rivals whose geographical location was like their own, and if pooling were improper or illegal, a strong position might prove not less useful in fighting." These earlier extensions also conduced markedly to economy of operation.

†From: U.S., Congress, House *Industrial Commission Reports*, 57th Cong., 1st sess., 1902, House Document No. 178, vol. 19, pp. 308-10.

Thus in place of the old fast freight lines which operated over a number of independent roads, a single railroad company could run its own cars without break directly from Chicago to the seaboard on its own rails. The object of these later consolidations is essentially different. The country has been well equipped with a network of branch lines and feeders. Most of the strategic points have been reached by a number of roads in common. There is no longer any object in economy of operation to be sought; in fact, the railroads since 1890 have been obliged to divide their lines into independent groups for operation separately, in order to obtain a maximum of economy. The new consolidations are intended expressly to obviate competition; once rival systems are brought under control in order to insure harmonious action. The railroads of the country are no longer divided into trunk lines and western systems, but the railroads east and west of Chicago and even west of the Missouri River are tending to become firmly knitted together.

A peculiarity of these recent changes deserves special mention. In order to attain a single important end it often becomes necessary to acquire an entire system of railroads, although only a small portion of that system can add directly to the efficiency of the controlling road. Thus, the entire Burlington system is absorbed by the northern transcontinental lines for no other reason than that they may obtain a direct entrance into Chicago. The Union Pacific Railroad purchased control of the Southern Pacific system, not because it needed that added mileage, but rather that it might indirectly acquire the Central Pacific and a direct outlet to the Pacific coast. The Long Island Railroad is purchased by the Pennsylvania Company, not for its local business along the main line, but simply in order that valuable terminals in Brooklyn may be developed. Even the profitable local business of the Central Railroad of New Jersey sinks into insignificance as a valuable possession of the Reading Railway when compared with its subsidiary coal business and the value of its terminals in Jersey City. This peculiarity of recent consolidations is undoubtedly due to the fact that the country is already sufficiently equipped with railroad lines for the transaction of ordinary business. New and independent inlets to strategic points would be therefore of doubtful value as self-supporting feeders. And more important still, terminal facilities have now become so valuable that no newly organized road or branch line can hope to secure an entrance without enormous cost. It may be cheaper, in other words, to buy a whole system for the sake of its terminals or for the sake of a part of its main line, than to develop new terminals or to parallel already existing railroads.

Undoubtedly the most important of the objects sought in these recent wholesale consolidations has been the elimination of competition; that is to say, to secure the maintenance of established rates by removal of the incentive to rate cutting which competition in the past has induced. In order to secure this end it has become practically necessary to dominate by one financial interest an entire geographical section of the country. This new policy of division of the field by means of community of interest deserves careful consideration by itself.

2

The Free Market vs. Regulation

Although the railroad bill passed by the House of Representatives did not reach the floor of the Senate in 1905, the Senate Commerce Committee did hold extensive hearings. The printed record of the hearings began with a summary of the basic argument involved over whether competition in the marketplace was sufficient to regulate rates. Most railroad leaders testified that while governmental regulation might be constitutional, it was not necessary.

Document†

ECONOMIC PRINCIPLES

Any discussion that brings into prominence the relation of government and industry is forced to place a comparative estimate upon two agencies for the control of industrial conduct. These agencies are voluntary association and governmental supervision. The former relies for efficiency upon the mutual interest of contracting parties; the latter brings into play all those familiar rules and maxims that are suggested by the term "public policy."

Those who rely upon the former believe that industry contains within itself means for the correction of the evils which its progress develops, while those who support the latter believe that the agencies of enlightened government can exercise a sufficiently intelligent and far-sighted control over business to enable the State to eliminate all evils of which complaint may justly be made and to promote general social welfare. The testimony submitted to the committee discloses a wide range of opinion so far as fundamental, industrial, and economic principles are concerned.

Those witnesses who oppose the further extension of statutory restraints upon the administration of railway properties argue that the commercial restraints are adequate, that competition, if not that of rival routes, at least that of markets and of consumers and producers, is both permanent and efficient, and that the public finds more effective protection against maladministration of railway property in the enlightened self-interest of railway officers and owners, on the one hand, and that of the traveling and shipping public on the other, than it could have at the hands of any administrative agency.

†From: U.S., Congress, Senate, Committee on Commerce, *Hearings on the Regulation of Railway Rates,* 59th Cong., 1st sess., 1906, Senate Document No. 243, vol. 1, pp. 11-16.

The advocates of further legislation, on the other hand, urge that the commercial restraints contemplated by the common law of industry fail to work satisfactorily when applied to the business of railway transportation, that the régime of free contract neither can nor does apply, and that there is frequently a conflict between the private interest of a railway corporation and the public interest of the community which the corporation serves. These divergent opinions are fundamental to the proper appreciation of the question under consideration and for that reason may be given somewhat at length.

The president of the Boston and Main Railroad says:

> Self-interest to the railroad is a governing factor in this matter. There is no mystery about the management of a railroad or its operation. Its business must be conducted upon exactly the same lines as any other trade or commercial business in the world. It depends for its life, for its income, upon the transportation of the property of its customers.

Another witness urges that "the principle of copartnership precludes anything of that sort"—that is to say, any disregard of the interest of the public and the shipper.

The president of the Great Northern Railroad says:

> You (that is to say, the railroad manager) must enable the man who lives on a farm, or works in the forest, or in the mines, to carry on his work with a profit or he will cease to work and your investment becomes worthless. * * * You are charged with the prosperity of every man on the line of the road, if he works.

Another form in which this same idea is presented is that there is nothing so peculiar about the manufacture and sale of transportation as to warrant the proposed treatment at the hands of Congress. The adjustment of rates through the agency of traffic officers, it is claimed, is an adjustment in response to natural law.

The president of the Delaware and Hudson Canal Company says:

> The transportation service is similar to any other service, and its price can not be successfully controlled by statute, but must depend on * * * natural laws. The most potent cause of the downward course of rates in the past has been not the statutes nor the Commission, but the pressing commercial necessities of shippers and consumers, and the efforts of traffic officials to meet them.

The president of the Illinois Central Railroad expresses his views as follows:

> We have had a free contest, so far, but under this bill (the Esch-Townsend bill) it is sought to put the power of fixing rates in the hands of a Government commission which is going to hamper the contest and bring in as controlling the situation, in lieu of supply and demand the world over, the *ipsi dixit* of a Government official.

The witness denies that traffic managers have any control over rates, as may be read from what follows:

> Senator NEWLANDS. The railroad companies do have some people, however, who fix these rates, do they not?
> Mr. FISH. They find a certain number of elements in the problem and then they work out the problem, that we can move a certain commodity at a certain rate; the conditions are such that in order to

move it it is necessary to do certain things, and we can do those things and meet those conditions then we contract to make that movement.

The CHAIRMAN. It is the conditions that govern?

Mr. FISH. The conditions govern.

The chairman of the trade and transportation committee of the New York Produce Exchange urges that railways—

> * * * Should be permitted to find their basis in the competition of the day, which from the nature of things must govern the carriers so long as they are free to establish the rates in the interest of territorial and industrial development, and upon which * * * the continued expansion of our commercial interests are primarily dependent.

One further quotation may be permitted, as it indicates the machinery through which the private interest of the corporations may become enlightened:

> There are several thousand of these general officers, and each of them has under him a large force of station agents and other employees to report to him and assist him in the proper performance of his work.
>
> These men are scattered throughout the country from one boundary to the other, and there is no place of any importance whatever that has not at least a station agent who is interested in the prosperity of his town, which necessarily involves the prosperity of its manufacturers and producers. He is, therefore, prepared to listen to any representation that these may make as to disadvantages which limit their business and as to proposed changes by which it could be increased. These are reported to the railroad headquarters, and it is the business of the head of the traffic department to give them prompt and careful consideration. Woe be to him if he does not! His position is naturally dependent upon his success in assisting in the development of the natural resources of his road. If the business does not increase, the railroad directors naturally look about for another man who knows how to bring about an increase, and the incompetent traffic man thus soon loses his place.

If the economic theory suggested by the above quotation approves itself to Congress (and this theory was expressed either directly or by implication by a large number of witnesses who appeared before the committee) it is evident that the current demand for further statutory restraint is both illogical and impolitic.

Not all the witnesses, however, subscribed to this theory of industrial control, although but few expressions in opposition to it are to be found. A member of the Interstate Commerce Commission expressed himself as follows:

> I do not know any other department of life, any other line of business, in which * * * the law-making power leaves the interest of one party * * * to the protection of the self-interest of the other party. It would hardly be assumed to be found a sound basis for the ascertainment and administration of justice anywhere else * * * that the rightful and lawful interest of one party to the transaction can be left for its protection to the self-interest of the other party.

The absence of more direct testimony against the doctrine of enlightened self-interest is not to be interpreted, however, as a concession on the part of the majority of witnesses that commercial considerations are an adequate guaranty of fair and equal relations between the railways and their patrons or of a wise administration of railway property from the public point of view.

The testimony contains many arguments and complaints that imply the contrary view. Frequent reference is made to the extent to which concentration of railway control has been carried by means of consolidations, contracts, and common understandings; a tendency in railway affairs which can have no bearing upon the problem in hand unless in support of the contention that these consolidations, contracts, and understandings have resulted in a virtual mastership of the situation by the railways and that this condition constitutes a monopoly power and exposes the shippers and the public to the possibility of an abuse of whatever power that monopoly gives.

The doctrine that private interest guarantees a just use of industrial property was developed as an essential part of English classical political economy at a time when normal competition, except as limited by law and custom, fairly controlled industrial conditions. But it is contended by all who demand that railway operations should be placed under unusual restraints that normal competition of the simple type no longer pertains to the situation under which American railways are administered. So far as this is admitted it becomes logically necessary for those who oppose legislative supervision to find a substitute for the old and simple type of competition in order to preserve vitality to the argument that when railways and their patrons seek their own respective interests they contribute in the highest practical degree to the collective interests of the community.

The substitute suggested in the testimony is what is termed "competition of the market" which presents itself in two forms. The first of these is found in the world's demand and the world's supply of commodities, and places reliance upon the fact that the necessity of participation by this country in the operations of the world's market is the ruling consideration for the adjustment of an important class of domestic rates. The second pertains to the domestic market, and is found in the struggle of producers and shippers in the various parts of the country to sell goods over as large a territory as possible and that of consumers to obtain their supplies at the lowest possible cost. This form of competition, it is claimed, is adequate to render the service under modern conditions which competition of the other sort was supposed to render by those publicists who developed the doctrine of enlightened self-interest.

The existence of this phase of competition is admitted by those who advocate legislative supervision over railways, but they claim that it is a vanishing force.

> Senator DOLLIVER. Do you mean to say that that kind of competition—that is to say, market competition between the Missouri Pacific and the Northwestern—in a case like that has disappeared?
>
> Mr. PROUTY. Certainly, I do, to a very great extent; I do not mean to say entirely. I do not mean to say it has disappeared to the same extent that competition in the rate has, because that, for all practical purposes, has absolutely disappeared in the United States. I do not pretend to say that competition in facilities, market competition, has disappeared, but I say it is disappearing.

This doctrine of enlightened self-interest was urged before the Senate committee of 1886, the report of which was made the basis of the "Act to regulate commerce" of 1887. The following is quoted from the Senate report of 1886 and indicates the conclusion to which the committee came at that time with regard to the line of argument made so prominent in the present testimony:

It is argued by railroad representatives that arbitrary or oppressive rates can not be maintained; that they are adjusted and sufficiently regulated by competition with rival roads and with water routes, by commercial necessities, by the natural laws of trade, and by that self-interest which compels the corporations to have due regard to the wants and the opinions of those upon whom they must depend for business; that such discriminations as exist are for the most part unavoidable; that the owners and managers of the property are the best judges of the conditions and circumstances that affect the cost of transportation and should determine the compensation they are entitled to receive; and that, in any event, the common law affords the shipper an adequate remedy and protection against abuse or any infringement of his rights. This answer fails to recognize the public nature and obligation of the carrier and the right of the people, through the governmental authority, to have a voice in the management of a corporation which performs a public function. Nor do the facts warrant the claim that competition and self-interest can be relied upon to secure the shipper against abuse and unjust discrimination, or that he has an available and satisfactory remedy at Common Law.

If it found that the Common Law and the courts do not in fact afford to the shipper an effective remedy for his grievance we have no need to inquire to what extent grievances may exist. The complicated nature of the countless transactions incident to the business of transportation makes it inevitable that disagreements should arise between the parties in interest, and it is neither just nor proper that disputed questions materially affecting the business operations of a shipper should be left in the final determination of those representing an opposing financial interest. When such disagreements occur the shipper and the carrier are alike entitled to a fair and impartial determination of the matters at issue, and by all the principles governing judicial proceedings the most fair-minded railroad official is disqualified by his personal interest in the result from giving such a determination.

It may have been true in 1887 that the doctrine of enlightened self-interest was advanced by the carriers in such a way as to amount to a denial of "the public nature and obligation of the carrier." No such denial appears in the present testimony. Witnesses on behalf of the railways have repeatedly admitted the right of public regulation and all of them have addressed their arguments soley to the question of expediency.

One view of the point which Congress is called upon to decide is expressed by the chairman of the Interstate Commerce Commission in discussing the importance to the country at large of the rate-making power. He says:

Do you realize what an enormous power that is putting into the hands of the railroads? That is the power of tearing down and building up. That is the power which might very largely control the distribution of industries, and I want to say in that connection that I think on the whole it is remarkable that that power has been so slightly abused. But it is there. My esteemed friend, Mr. Elliott, has just told you that the rates on wool from Montana must be adjusted with reference to the rates on wool from Kentucky. Well, grant it. But suppose he should see fit to adjust his rates on wool so that they moved to the Pacific coast and it became for the interest of his railroad to change the adjustment. Is that to be left entirely to his judgment? After all, are the railroads to be left virtually free to make such rates as they conceive to be in their interests? Undoubtedly their interest in large measure and for the most part is the interest of the communities they serve. Undoubtedly in large measure and for the most part they try as honestly and as con-scientiously as men can to make fair adjustments of their charges. But suppose they do not. Is there not to be any redress for those who suffer? That is really the question.

It is not possible to entertain a consistent opinion relative to remedial legislation, such as is now pressed upon the attention of Congress, without assuming a definite point of view with regard to the extent to which reliance may be placed upon commercial conditions and commercial forces in the regulation and control of railway operations, as well as upon the wisdom and precision with which remedies involving the exercise of political power can be applied.

3

A Menace to the Freedom of Commerce

James J. Hill, E.H. Harriman, and J.P. Morgan combined the Great Northern, the Northern Pacific, and the Chicago, Burlington & Quincy into an enormous holding company called Northern Securities, which controlled the northern routes from Chicago to the Pacific Coast. Theodore Roosevelt's administration attacked the combination as a monopolistic violation of the Sherman Act, and the Supreme Court agreed.

Document†

The Government charges that if the combination was held not to be in violation of the act of Congress, then all efforts of the National Government to preserve to the people the benefits of free competition among carriers engaged in interstate commerce will be wholly unavailing, and all transcontinental lines, indeed the entire railway systems of the country, may be absorbed, merged and consolidated, thus placing the public at the absolute mercy of the holding corporation.

The several defendants denied all the allegations of the bill imputing to them a purpose to evade the provisions of the act of Congress, or to form a combination or conspiracy having for its object either to restrain or to monopolize commerce or trade among the States or with foreign nations. They denied that any combination or conspiracy was formed in violation of the act.

In our judgment, the evidence fully sustains the material allegations of the bill, and shows a violation of the act of Congress, in so far as it declares illegal every combination or conspiracy in restraint of commerce among the several States and with foreign nations, and forbids attempts to monopolize such commerce or any part of it.

Summarizing the principal facts, it is indisputable upon this record that under the leadership of the defendants Hill and Morgan the stockholders of the Great Northern and Northern Pacific Railway corporations, having competing and substantially parallel lines from the Great Lakes and the Mississippi River to the Pacific Ocean at Puget Sound combined and conceived the scheme of organizing a corporation under the laws of New Jersey, which should *hold* the shares of the stock of the constituent

†From: *Northern Securities Company v. United States,* 193 U.S. 197 (1904), in *Federal Antitrust Decisions* (Washington, D.C.: Government Printing Office, 1907), vol. 2, pp. 486-88.

companies, such shareholders, in lieu of their shares in those companies, to receive, upon an agreed basis of value, shares in the holding corporation; that pursuant to such combination the Northern Securities Company was organized as the holding corporation through which the scheme should be executed; and under that scheme such holding corporation has become the holder—more properly speaking, the custodian—of more than nine-tenths of the stock of the Northern Pacific, and more than three-fourths of the stock of the Great Northern, the stockholders of the companies who delivered their stock receiving upon the agreed basis shares of stock in the holding corporation. The stockholders of these two competing companies disappeared, as such, for the moment, but immediately reappeared as stockholders of the holding company which was thereafter to guard the interests of both sets of stockholders as a unit, and to manage, or cause to be managed, both lines of railroad as if held *in one ownership*. Necessarily by this combination or arrangement the holding company in the fullest sense dominates the situation in the interest of those who were stockholders of the constituent companies; as much so, for every practical purpose, as if it had been itself a railroad corporation which had built, owned, and operated both lines for the exclusive benefit of its stockholders. Necessarily, also, the constituent companies ceased, under such a combination, to be in active competition for trade and commerce along their respective lines, and have become, practically, one powerful consolidated corporation, by the name of a holding corporation the principal, if not the sole, object for the formation of which was to carry out the purpose of the original combination under which competition between the constituent companies would cease. Those who were stockholders of the Great Northern and Northern Pacific and became stockholders in the holding company are now interested in preventing all competition between the two lines, and as owners of stock or of certificates of stock in the holding company, they will see to it that no competition is tolerated. They will take care that no persons are chosen directors of the holding company who will permit competition between the constituent companies. The result of the combination is that all the earnings of the constituent companies make a common fund in the hands of the Northern Securities Company to be distributed, not upon the basis of the earnings of the respective constituent companies, each acting exclusively in its own interest, but upon the basis of the certificates of stock issued by the holding company. No scheme or device could more certainly come within the words of the act—"combination in the form of a trust or otherwise * * * in restraint of commerce among the several States or with foreign nations,"—or could more effectively and certainly suppress free competition between the constituent companies. This combination is, within the meaning of the act, a "trust;" but if not, it is a *combination in restraint of interstate and international commerce*; and that is enough to bring it under the condemnation of the act. The mere existence of such a combination and the power acquired by the holding company as its trustee, constitute a menace to, and a restraint upon, that freedom of commerce which Congress intended to recognize and protect, and which the public is entitled to have protected. If such combination be not destroyed, all the advantages that would naturally come to the public under the operation of the general laws of competition, as between the Great Northern and Northern Pacific Railway companies, will be lost, and the entire commerce of the immense territory in the northern part of the United States between the Great Lakes and the Pacific at Puget Sound will be at the mercy of a single holding corporation, organized in a State distant from the people of that territory.

The Circuit Court was undoubtedly right when it said—all the Judges of that court concurring—that the combination referred to "led inevitably to the following results: First, it placed the control of the two roads in the hands of a single person, to wit, the Securities Company, by virtue of its ownership of a large majority of the stock of both companies; second, it destroyed every motive for competition between two roads engaged in interstate traffic, which were natural competitors for business, by pooling the earnings of the two roads for the common benefit of the stockholders of both companies." 120 Fed. Rep. 721, 724.

4

Senate Debate Over Railroad Regulation

In a spirited debate, Democratic Senators Alexander Clay (Georgia), Joseph Bailey (Texas), and "Pitchfork" Ben Tillman (South Carolina) expressed their conviction that the Republicans Joseph Foraker (Ohio) and Senate "Boss" Nelson W. Aldrich (Rhode Island) were determined to oppose any effectual governmental regulation of the railroads.

Document†

Mr. FORAKER. I wish to ask the Senator from Georgia a question. I have been trying for a good while to do it, and I think that now is a good place.

Mr. CLAY. I would like to ask the Senator, does he contend that he has not asked me a question before?

Mr. FORAKER. Oh, I have asked the Senator several questions, but not anything like as many as I have been disposed to ask him. But I did not want to interrupt him. I do not want the Senator to think that because I have been sitting here listening in silence to most of his speech that I believe there is very much in it. He will therefore permit me to say I do not.

I understood the Senator to say that he favors this proposition, among other reasons, because it will save us from Government ownership. I wanted to ask the Senator right here whether he can tell us of any man in all this country who is in favor of Government ownership who is not in favor of this proposition?

Mr. CLAY. I beg to say that I have never been close to the political party in favor of Government ownership or the public men who advocated Government ownership. I do not know how those who favor Government ownership feel in regard to Government regulation. I may be mistaken about it, but I believe that 75 per cent of the American people are in favor of clothing the Interstate Commerce Commission with power to investigate complaints and to fix reasonable and just rates.

Mr. BAILEY. Mr. President——

Mr. ALDRICH. Now I will yield to the Senator from Texas.

Mr. BAILEY. Mr. President, the Senator from Rhode Island and all other Senators know how much I deprecate making a partisan issue over any question. On this side we give evidence of our willingness to forego party advantage when we permit a Republican President to take bodily from our

†From: U.S., Congress, Senate, *Congressional Record*, 59th Cong., 1st sess., 1906, vol. 40, pt. 2, pp. 1364-65.

national platform an important plank and make it as his recommendation to Congress without a syllable of complaint. We manifest not only a willingness but an eagerness to vote for it, and it comes with bad grace from that side when a Senator on this side espouses the policy of the President for a distinguished Republican leader to rebuke him by an allusion to a Democrat [Congressman William Randolph Hearst] who happens not to be popular with the Senator from Rhode Island or those who think with him. That particular Democrat may or may not be popular on this side of the Chamber. Some of his views are undoubtedly rejected. Some of his views, I have no doubt, would receive a cordial support.

I doubt if there is any man in this country claiming to be a Democrat and of sufficient prominence to make it worth while to consider what he says or does who does not advocate some measure acceptable to all of us. One measure might be acceptable to gentlemen on the other side, another measure might be acceptable to those on this side, and it would be no just ground of criticism from us against you or from you against us that on a particular measure he concurs with us.

But I rose merely to ask, in a spirit of absolute nonpartisanship, why the Senator from Rhode Island and his associates can not agree upon a bill substantially in the very words of the President's message? That the Senator from Rhode Island does not accept the wisdom of a Republican President is not strange to us who know the Senator or who know the President. The Senator from Rhode Island is nothing if not conservative. The President of the United States is nothing if not emotional. It is utterly impossible to conceive two characters so wholly dissimilar as the Senator from Rhode Island and the President of the United States. And yet I must assume that both the President of the United States and the Senator from Rhode Island want to do equal and exact justice both to the railroads and to the shipper.

Now, if the Senator from Rhode Island is willing to maintain before the Senate and in the presence of the country that a bill along the lines so earnestly and so ably advocated by the Senator from Georgia will not do justice, then I recommend that he settle his quarrel within his own party, beginning this adjustment with the President of the United States himself.

Mr. ALDRICH. Mr. President, I regret as much as the Senator from Texas possibly can the injection of partisanship into this discussion. I certainly am not the guilty party.

Mr. TILLMAN. You are the very man.

Mr. ALDRICH. It was the Senator from Georgia who begged us to save the country from a leading Democrat whose position to-day is so overshadowing that there is hardly a man on this side of the Chamber or that who does not believe either he or Mr. Bryan will lead the Democratic party in the next national campaign. I deprecate, I say again, as much as the Senator from Texas can that the discussion has taken any such direction. I say we have had fully shown the spirit of the Senator from Georgia, which led him for reasons of his own to bring into this discussion a personality which might be used, in his judgment, to frighten this side and that from doing what they think might otherwise be their duty. But that is not what I arose to say. The Senator from Georgia——

Mr. BAILEY. Will the Senator from Rhode Island permit me?

Mr. ALDRICH. Certainly.

Mr. BAILEY. The Senator has been good enough to tell us who will be the Democratic nominee at the next Presidential election. Will he now be good enough to tell us who is to be the Republican nominee?

Mr. ALDRICH. There is no such consensus of opinion in Republican circles as there is in Democratic, I am happy to say.

Mr. BAILEY. We are not altogether a harmonious family, but the only difference between us and you is that we speak our differences a little louder than you do. The differences in the Republican party are to-day more violent than they are with us. I do not invite you to discuss those differences in public; but having volunteered to inform the country in advance whom we would nominate—and I am free to say that if we knew what you wanted us to do we would be certain to do the other thing if we are rational—it seems to me the Senator, who professes to know so much about our party, ought to know something about his own, and I should like to have him state what he thinks of the publication in this morning's paper that the President is to be a candidate for a third term upon a platform "against the money power."

Mr. ALDRICH. Mr. President, there was just one serious point in the speech of the Senator from Georgia which I can not overlook. He states that the entire railroad interests of the country are controlled by six different groups of interests.

Mr. CLAY. Mr. President, I read the testimony of an Interstate Commerce Commissioner.

Mr. ALDRICH. Yes; that is right. Now, if I understand the logic of his argument, it is that there is but very little competition now existing in rates or facilities for transportation in the United States, on account of the fact that all the railroad business of the country is concentrated in a few hands. Now, what does he propose as a remedy? He proposes to consolidate every mile of railroad in the United States in one combination. He proposes to give into the hands of a commission arbitrary power to fix every railroad rate in the United States and to destroy beyond any power of recovery every vestige of competition; to create, in other words, one great railroad combination.

Mr. CLAY. Will the Senator yield to me right there?

Mr. ALDRICH. No; let me finish the sentence.

The VICE-PRESIDENT. The Senator from Rhode Island refuses to yield.

Mr. ALDRICH. I will in just a minute. He proposes to put in place of six great influential railroad combinations one monster combination, under Government control and Government regulation, with no power to change rates on the part of anybody after they are once established by the Commission and ratified by the courts. He proposes to destroy the last vestige by law in the name of Democracy and in the name of the people. He proposes to wipe out what there is left of possible competition in transportation, and by what would be an infamous project give one commission, without appeal and without review except upon some unimportant collaterial questions, the arbitrary power to fix rates, not alone for the railroads, but for the shipper, for you and me, and every man in the country who would thus be made to bow down to this monster who would have in its clutch the great business interests of this country, put there by your votes—you who speak or pretend to speak in the name of Democracy and the people.

Mr. CLAY. Mr. President, the Senator from Rhode Island has said that I stated in my argument that I desire to place arbitrary power in the hands of the Interstate Commerce Commission to fix rates, and without any appeal from the decisions of that Commission, whether those rates were reasonable or not.

Mr. ALDRICH. Oh, no; I did not say quite that.

Mr. CLAY. I think I heard the Senator.

Mr. ALDRICH. I said the power to fix rates which when once approved by the courts could not possibly be changed.

Mr. CLAY. Why, Mr. President, the Senator knows well that the Interstate Commerce Commission during the ten years it exercised that power frequently changed the rates the Commission had already made. No Commission ought to be permitted to make a rate that shall stand for all time. Different circumstances may arise; different conditions may arise; and the Commission ought to be empowered to lower or increase the rate if different conditions should arise. Now, let us see——

Mr. ALDRICH. But——

Mr. CLAY. Let me get through. Mr. President, all I propose to do is simply to say to the Commission, "You shall do right;" that the Commission shall say to the railroads, "You shall do right. You shall make reasonable and just rates. If you do, they stand; if not, they will be set aside." And, Mr. President, the Attorney-General has joined the Democratic party on that line. The Republican party has joined the Democratic party on that line. Convention after convention, chamber of commerce after chamber of commerce, has joined the Democratic party on that line. But what says the Senator from Rhode Island? Railroads draw out of the pockets of the people $2,000,000,000 for passenger fares and freights every year. Shall the roads continue to fix the rates and the shippers have nowhere to go to make their complaints and redress their wrongs? Must the shipper be bound by the rates fixed by the roads, whether reasonable or unreasonable, and will the Republican party leave the law in this condition? Is that the position of the Senator from Rhode Island?

Mr. ALDRICH. I made no such suggestion.

Mr. CLAY. I am not through yet.

The VICE-PRESIDENT. The Senator from Georgia declines to yield.

Mr. CLAY. I will yield in one minute.

Mr. President, the Senator from Rhode Island says that nothwithstanding the fact that the railroads exercise the right of eminent domain, that they can condemn our homes and our farms, and that is right and proper, and notwithstanding the fact that they get their life from the State and the

Government he denies to Congress the right to give to any tribunal the right to hear the complaint of the shipper, even though the rate fixed by the roads may be ever so unreasonable and unjust. He says, "Be silent; stand right where you are." He has offered no remedy. Mr. President, he has said that the roads ought to fix their own rates, and whether reasonable or unreasonable these rates ought to stand. He suggests no remedy. He belongs to that part of his party that believes in letting well enough alone, and says there shall be no interference; that a citizen shall have nowhere to go if the roads confiscate his property; if they destroy private industries, then the citizen is without any remedy. The railroads doubtless will agree with the Senator from Rhode Island, but I doubt if the American people will approve his doctrine.

Mr. ALDRICH. The Senator from Georgia in the last ten minutes has been undertaking to express my opinion, when I have carefully abstained from expressing one single suggestion as to my own position. I have not stated, directly or indirectly, what my judgment or idea is in regard to this subject, and his statement in that connection is entirely a figment of his own imagination. I have made no statement of any kind as to my own views about this matter.

I was trying to conduct, I trust modestly, an inquiry into the arguments presented by the Senator from Georgia to test their validity and their logic, and to make such suggestions in connection with them as seemed to me to be wise. I am a member of the Interstate Commerce Committee and in a certain sense a judge with reference to all these questions. I will speak sooner or later and will be able to show the Senate, both by vote and voice, what my position is. In the meantime I shall ask the Senator from Georgia to excuse me if I do not make him my mouthpiece, and do not accept his utterances as official as far as I am concerned.

5

With Contempt for the Regulators

James J. Hill, builder of the Great Northern and a partner of J.P. Morgan, was one of the ablest of the railroad magnates and a plainspoken man. In testifying before the Elkins Committee, he expressed his contempt for government regulators.

Document†

Mr. HILL. Well, now, Senator, I am a firm believer in all natural laws where we have demonstrated that they are laws, and the law of the survival of the fittest is a natural law that we can safely adopt. I think I would let a railway company consider the investment; I would protect the property as I would any other property, and I would hold them for their good behavior, as I would everybody else. If the railway company can make the rate and can do it profitably, give them an opportunity to do it. Do not say, "You must make good this man's mistakes." If I build a factory to-day, or buy one that is out of date, with machinery 25 or 30 years old, and my neighbor comes in and builds a factory with modern machinery and he can produce the cloth for 10 or 15 per cent less than I can produce it for, would I not look strange to go and ask him to divide his profit with me? That is what a great many raidways ask, and a great many people think it would be an advantage to the country to allow the railways to make pools. My theory is: Hold them to a strict observance of the law and enforce it, and let them have room according to their heft. Let them have room to see what they can do, what they will do; nothing else ever brought our rates down.

Senator FORAKER. You have said somebody ought to go and buy the Erie Railroad. That was your expression?

Mr. HILL. I said somebody could.

Senator FORAKER. Then, if somebody were to go and buy it, it would be necessary to make a trunk line out of it?

Mr. HILL. It is a trunk line. It could be improved.

Senator FORAKER. You say it is a "flintlock" road——

Mr. HILL. Well, it could be improved.

Senator FORAKER (continuing). And a muzzle-loader?

Mr. HILL. It could be improved.

†From: U.S., Congress, Senate, Committee on Interstate Commerce, *Hearings on the Regulation of Railway Rates,* 59th Cong., 1st sess., 1906, Senate Document No. 243, vol. 2, p. 1481.

Senator FORAKER. I am using your expressions.

Mr. HILL. I say it could be improved.

Senator FORAKER. And you would expect it to be?

Mr. HILL. Yes, sir.

Senator FORAKER (continuing). If anybody should buy it who wanted to do business in competition?

Mr. HILL. Yes. It would take some money. But, you see, there is the point: Who will put the money in, when every dollar that is invested is threatened with having the control of it taken away and handed over to some sort of a commission, whom we know, who have to deal with them, are absolutely incompetent? With all due deference to the men on that Commission—I have a high regard for many of them—what position could they fill on a railway? I do not know any. We pay traffic men thirty to forty thousand, and as high as $50,000 a year, because they are worth it.

6

How Wisconsin Regulated the Railroads

Robert M. La Follette battled his way to the Governorship of Wisconsin on a pledge properly to regulate and tax the railroads. The law that he fought through the legislature was generally considered to be a model of effective state regulation.

Document†

The La Follette Railroad Law in Wisconsin
By JOHN R. COMMONS.
(Professor of Political Economy in the University of Wisconsin.)

WHEN the record of the Wisconsin Legislature of 1905 is summed up it will show a series of enactments remarkable in their union of progressivism and conservatism. This is especially true of the law regulating railway charges and services. The Legislature and the governor, as is well known, were elected on this issue, after a campaign national in the interest aroused. This campaign, with its split in the Republican party and its new alignment of voters, was the culmination of a struggle extending through the past ten years and marked during preceding legislative sessions by an anti-pass law, a law taxing railway companies on the full value of their property, and a primary-election law. . . . The purpose of the present article is to analyze the railway law just passed, to point out its significant features, and to indicate both its likeness and unlikeness to similar laws in other States, and the reasons advanced therefor.

Wisconsin was one of the four "Granger" States, which in the early seventies revolutionized the policies of the State governments toward railways. The "Potter" law of 1874 was similar to laws enacted in the same year in Iowa and Minnesota, and in 1871 in Illinois. These laws created State railway commissions, with power to fix maximum rates. Coming, as they did, in the midst of an industrial panic and depression, and being admittedly crude and novel, the railway companies were able, in 1876, to secure their repeal in all of the Granger States except Illinois. The agitation, however, was renewed, and, following the year when the interstate-commerce law was enacted, the States of Iowa and Minnesota returned to the policy of 1874-76. A similar bill, [was] introduced in the Wisconsin Legislature in 1889, ... but was defeated. It came up again in legislative sessions during the nineties, but was

†From: *The American Monthly Review of Reviews*, vol. 32 (July, 1905), pp. 76-79.

again defeated. It was then held in abeyance by Governor La Follette and his supporters until the anti-pass, taxation, and primary-election laws could be disposed of. Finally, in the session of 1903, following the governor's message on the subject, a bill was again introduced, but after a heated discussion in and out of the Legislature, including a second and special message from the governor, it was defeated in the Assembly. The record of that Legislature and of the governor became the issue of 1904, and there has perhaps never been an act of State legislation so eagerly studied by all the people, with such masses of statistics, and such detailed comparisons with other States, as the revised and amended law of 1905, which came out of the proposed law of 1903. That bill was modeled after the law of Iowa, but the law of 1905 profits by the experiences of all the States, and by many decisions of the State and federal courts. Compared with other laws, it is less sweeping and radical at some points, but more strongly bulwarked at others.

An Appointive Commission

This is seen in the importance attached to the provisions for selecting the three State railroad commissioners, and in the grant of large powers, with wide discretion in the use of those powers. Both of these features are a reversal of the tendency shown in other States. The salary of each commissioner is fixed at $5,000, a sum more than double that of the Iowa commissioners and 40 per cent greater than that of the Illinois commissioners. . . . The terms of the commissioners are six years, one to be appointed each alternate year. Of course, the object in view is to keep the commission from falling into the hands of the railways, and to avoid such an outcome as that in Iowa, for example, where the commission is notoriously reputed, throughout Wisconsin, at least, to be composed of three men nominated, respectively, by the three great railway systems of that State. The contest on this point turned mainly on the method of selection, whether by popular election or by governor's appointment. It is quite noteworthy that the railways contended for election, while the governor and the legislative majority were for appointment; and this notwithstanding the example of nine States which have changed from appointive to elective commissions, leaving only six of the States that regulate rates with appointive commissions, against sixteen with elective commissions. More especially is this reversal of the trend in other States noteworthy since Wisconsin, under the leadership of Governor La Follette, has just adopted a comprehensive primary-election law designed for the very purpose of preventing the corporation from controlling party conventions and elective officers. . . .

The Roads Still Free to Make Special Rates

These duties and powers are stated in the broadest terms, with very little that is mandatory and very much that is discretionary. In the first place, a break again is made away from the trend in other States, in that the commission is not required to fix a classification of goods or a schedule of all rates to be charged, but is authorized to review any or all rates made by the roads, and then, after a full hearing, to substitute a reasonable rate. The commission does not lay down any rule for arriving at a tariff, but takes into account every element that has a bearing or influence on the rate. The law in this respect is less radical than other recent legislation, for in twelve years the number of States in which the commission *must* make complete schedules of freight rates for each railroad has increased from seven to thirteen, while the number in which the commission *may* make specific rates has decreased from eight to seven.

. . . By leaving the initiative to the roads, they are free, as before, to adapt their rates to industrial conditions, but the commission is at hand to check their acts if they are unjustly discriminatory. The roads can even make non-compensatory rates in order to stimulate business and increase other forms of traffic if they see fit to do so,—an act which, if ordered by a State commission, would be overruled by the courts.

One feature of the law which, however, is the same as that in sixteen of the twenty States that regulate rates is the power of the commission to fix an absolute rate rather than to declare what shall be a maximum rate. It thus is made unlawful as much for the company to charge less than the commission rate as to charge more than that rate. This naturally follows from the intention to prevent unjust discrimination between shippers and com- munities,—an object equally important with that of preventing excessive charges.

Rates Must Be Proved Unreasonable Before Action is Taken

The theory of the new law seems to be that the railroads have their experts with years of experience in making rates and handling traffic; but that no body of men, however expert, can be trusted in all cases and at all times to use their uncontrolled power, upon which the wealth and prosperity of the State depends, in a manner fair and reasonable. On the other hand, no body of men selected by the State can have the expert qualifications and the detailed information that come from daily contact with the problems. On this account, the rates made by the railroads are in effect held to be, *prima facie*, reasonable and lawful. This is a radical distinction from the laws in those States which require the commission to fix a complete schedule of rates, the evident assumption there being that the road's rates are, *prima facie*, unlawful and unreasonable.

These rates in Wisconsin, however, may be challenged, but the burden of proof is upon the complainant to show that they are unreasonable. The railroad commission is the board of review to investigate the complaint, with all the powers over witnesses, books, and testimony intrusted to a court of record. It gives the railroad company and the complainant ten days' notice of a hearing; upon which, if it find proof that the rate is "unreasonable or unjustly discriminatory," it fixes a reasonable rate, and its order takes effect of its own force in twenty days after service on the railway officer. Thenceforth, the legal situation is reversed. The rates fixed by the commission now in turn become, *prima facie*, lawful and reasonable, and the burden of proof is upon the railway company if it goes into court and asks that they be overruled. Upon the several steps involved in these provisions the contest in the Senate committee, where the principal struggle occured, was prolonged and intense, and it is most remarkable that, starting with opposing views, that committee reported a bill unanimously which then was unanimously adopted by both houses and signed by the governor.

The first step in the controversy related to the source of complaint against the rates or regulations of the roads. The companies contended that only shippers were affected, and that they only should be entitled to enter complaint. But it was shown that public interests were involved, and that localities might be injuriously affected. Consequently, the law entertains complaints "of any person, firm, corporation, or association, or of any mercantile, agricultural, or manufacturing society, or of any body politic or municipal organization." A railroad itself is permitted to make complaint against another railroad, and there is nothing in the law to prevent the commission from raising the rates of a road that is resorting to a destructive rate war.

The Commission Itself May Take The Initiative

Next, the railroads, continuing the idea that the commission should be a quasi-judicial body, held that, conceding that it might decide on complaints, it should not itself initiate investigations. But the committee decided that the commission should be actually, what the courts have supported legally, an arm of the Legislature, and gave it power, "upon its own motion," to investigate any rate or charge. It thus becomes the organ, as stated by the governor, "of the great body of the people of Wisconsin, who bear in the aggregate the principal burden of the freight rates," but who "could not appear before the commission to make complaint," nor "state their complaint or allege the measure of the wrong imposed upon them." The procedure, when initiation is by the commission, is the same as when a complaint is made. . . .

The Railroads and the Courts

. . . By the procedure adopted the commission's rates are, *prima facie*, lawful, the burden of proof is upon the railroad, and the court passes upon the lawfulness of the rate itself exactly as it would pass upon the constitutionality of a statute. The commission retains its rights as a legislative arm, and the court acts in its strictly judicial capacity of determining, under the constitution, whether the commission has exceeded its powers in establishing a rate that is unreasonable,—that is, unlawful. . . .

A Comprehensive Enactment

There are miscellaneous features of the law which can only be mentioned. It, of course, prohibits rebates and discrimination, provides for inquiry into violations, for prosecutions and penalties, thus giving the commission power to enforce its orders. It covers passenger service as well as freight service. It includes express companies, private-car companies, refrigerator lines, sleeping-car companies, and interurban electric lines. It controls all rules and regulations, switching charges, and so on, that in any manner affect the charge for transportation. It requires reasonably adequate service and facilities. It gives the commission power to require accounts, and especially "copies of all contracts which relate to the transportation of persons or property, or any service in connection therewith, made or entered into by it with any other railroad company, car company, equipment company, express or transportation company, or any shipper or shippers, or other person or persons doing business with it." It requires to be filed with the commission a verified list of all passes, tickets, or mileage books issued free or for less than the full established rates in cash, together with the names of recipients and the amounts received and the reasons for issuing them. The commission may employ experts and fix their compensation, and is required to determine the cost of construction and the value of physical properties, as well as various details regarding indebtedness, wages and hours of labor, and accidents. These and the other provisions described place the commission in the possession of accurate knowledge of all facts pertaining to the Wisconsin business of the roads, with both the weapon of publicity and the reserve power of compulsion.

7

La Follette on Railroad Misbehavior

Senator La Follette believed that the Hepburn Act would not give the Interstate Commerce Commission enough power properly to regulate the railroads. In private conference with President Roosevelt and on the floor of the Senate, he sought to strengthen it. La Follette particularly wanted consumer interests protected and rates set on the basis of the actual reproduction value of railroad properties, instead of on their often highly inflated stock and bond issues. At first other members of the Senate walked out, leaving him speaking to the galleries and empty Senate seats, but he was able to draw them back. Republican Senators Jonathan Dolliver of Iowa, who was guiding the bill, and Albert J. Beveridge of Indiana later became the core of La Follette's group of Progressive Republican reformers.

Document†

Mr. DOLLIVER. Mr. President—

The VICE-PRESIDENT. Does the Senator from Wisconsin yield to the Senator from Iowa?

Mr. LA FOLLETTE. Certainly.

Mr. DOLLIVER. Consultation with the members of the Interstate Commerce Commission has led me to believe that with their power of investigating general rate conditions throughout the country, if they discover an abuse they will be under no inconvenience whatever under the provisions of section 15 in founding a proper complaint.

Mr. LA FOLLETTE. Mr. President, I noticed in the discussion in the House of Representatives that the member from one of the Maine districts raised that question and objected that there were provisions in this bill which might be so construed as to allow the Commission to issue an order upon the investigation which it had made on its own motion under section 13. I observed that a member of the House committee which framed the bill promptly declared that such construction could not be given to it.

Mr. DOLLIVER. I think the Senator from Wisconsin will agree with me that if we can secure an adjudication of every complaint that may be filed, we will have gone a long way toward curing, or at least securing jurisdiction of, most railroad abuses.

†From: U.S., Congress, Senate, *Congressional Record*, 59th Cong., 1st sess., 1906, vol. 40, pt. 6, pp. 5695, 5702, 5716, 5721.

Mr. LA FOLLETTE. I am sorry to disagree with my friend the Senator from Iowa. I think we shall have gone only a *very little* way. Under the provisions of this bill I do not think we will go to the heart of this problem at all. I believe I shall be able to make this very clear, if Senators have the patience to hear me to the end.

If consumers are to be greatly benefited by securing even relatively reasonable rates, it would seem very clear that either the Commission should be authorized to act upon its own motion or the Government should provide some agency authorized to make preliminary investigation into the wrongs suffered by the consumers, file complaints, and prosecute the same before the Commission. Some communities and rural sections might, thus aided, secure at least a moiety of relief.

The whole history of this struggle for legislation, reaching back more than a score of years, reveals the fact that those who are strong through the power of organization and wealth fare the best.

Mr. President, it is on this broad ground of a just protection of public interest that the proposed bill seems to me narrow and far below the level demanded by experienced and enlightened public judgment. It is only designed to be amendatory of the law passed twenty years ago. In some respects it is less effective than the original law was believed to be by those who enacted it—by the public and railroad companies as well.

... Mr. President, I think perhaps I ought to say that it is my personal belief that not only the junior Senator from Iowa [Mr. Dolliver], but many other Senators, when they come, as they will come, because of their interest in this important subject, to consider every phase of it, as bearing on the welfare of the people of this country, will be found standing for that which the interests of this country demand.

I recall, in the course of the eloquent and able address delivered early in the debate by the Senator from Iowa, the statement, which may have escaped others, but which I noted, that his opinions with respect to this question, though perhaps it was more particularly with respect to the Commission itself, had undergone somewhat of a change in the last year or so. I am sure that he approaches this question to-day with an open mind.

When any man who cares for his country comes to realize the true significance of the control of commerce upon the development of all industry, the location of markets, the building of cities, the density of population, the tremendous influence upon the economic and social life of the people, with all its consequence to this generation and the generations to come, he will be shocked that it should all be left in the hands of the traffic managers of railroads. The control of commerce—its regulation, its rates, its distribution and destination—go to the upbuilding of the State, the nation. It must be controlled unselfishly, controlled with the highest patriotism, upon a broad, national policy.

When this idea is once grasped, when it once possesses the American people, does the Senate believe, does anyone believe that they will permit the destiny of this nation to be controlled by a board of managers of consolidated railways?

Sir, I say to the Senate here to-day that nothing, *absolutely nothing*, can prevent the ultimate government ownership of the railroads of this country except a strict government control of the railroads of the country. [Manifestations of applause in the galleries.]

The VICE-PRESIDENT. The Senator from Wisconsin will suspend while the Chair warns the occupants of the galleries against further violation of the rules of the Senate, which forbid applause or demonstrations in the galleries. The Senator from Wisconsin will proceed.

... If a railroad line has had issued bonds and stocks away in excess of the investment of the fair value of the property, the public can not justly be taxed to pay dividends upon stock and interest upon bonds thus issued. In other words, the old rule that puts every man when he makes a purchase upon his inquiry as to the value of the property he purchases requires that the man buying stocks and bonds shall know whether there is back of those stocks and bonds in which he invests his money that value which is specified on their face.

Mr. BEVERIDGE. If the Senator will permit me further, it would strike me right here that in the matter of fixing railway rates would come the question of just compensation, or even of confiscation.

Mr. TILLMAN. We are interested in this discussion, and I suggest that the Senator from Indiana raise his voice a little.

Mr. BEVERIDGE. I will.

Mr. TILLMAN. And that he change his position so that his voice will be sidewise to us instead of his back being to us. We should like to hear what he is saying.

Mr. BEVERIDGE. I was addressing the Senator from Wisconsin. However, I will try to comply with the suggestion of the Senator from South Carolina.

Suppose that here is the overcapitalization to which the Senator refers, and rates are based upon it in order to pay dividends upon that capitalization. This overcapitalization has been absorbed by the innocent purchasing public. Upon the theory that the railroads should charge rates which would pay a fair return upon the actual just value of the road no dividends whatever would be paid upon the overcapitalization. Therefore, when such rates were fixed, the road would at once say "this is the taking of property without just compensation." That is the point to which I wish to direct the Senator's attention.

Mr. LA FOLLETTE. In response to that question the Supreme Court would say, as it has said heretofore, that it is not required of the public to pay dividends and interest on water, no matter who owns it, but that it shall pay dividends and interest on the fair value of the property, and nothing more. The Supreme Court has said that if any railroad company has issued stock and bonds in excess of the fair value of its property it must suffer, and those who hold the stock and bonds must suffer the consequences of such action; that it is unjust to impose that burden upon the public. If railroad companies are to be permitted to issue stocks and bonds without limit, if there is to be no restriction whatever, and none has been imposed except in the state of Texas, so far as I am advised—

Mr. DOLLIVER. And Massachusetts.

Mr. LA FOLLETTE. Massachusetts; yes. There is State regulation in Massachusetts, but with these exceptions the directors of a railroad company may, without any limitation whatever, burden the public with transportation charges to pay interest and dividends, not upon capital invested in the business of transportation, but upon any figure they choose to put upon the paper certificates they issue.

... Mr. President, the railroad is entitled to "just compensation" for its public services.

Reasonable rates are held to be such rates as afford "just compensation."

The Supreme Court has determined that reasonable rates affording "just compensation" are such rates as pay a fair return on a fair value of railway property.

We shall settle nothing then, respecting reasonable rates and just compensation until we ascertain the fair value of the railroad property of the country.

The railroads are capitalized at $13,213,124,679 (1904).

The public believes that this capitalization grossly exceeds the fair value of the property; that it has been wrongfully "watered" and inflated; and that the producers and consumers of the country are unjustly taxed on transportation to pay an income upon a false and fradulent valuation. The railroads deny this claim. That makes a sharp and conflicting issue between the public and the railroads.

I shall, therefore, present in this connection evidence of the over capitalization, inflation, and "watering" of many of the railroad properties of the country. I shall go into the subject fully enough to impeach the standing capitalization of the railroad property of the country. I shall present such an array of facts as shall enforce the public demand for an accurate valuation of the railroad property of the country. . . .

Conclusion

Sir, this extended review of the evidence of increasing rates and vicious discrimination, of the methods of railroad building, overcapitalization, and reckless speculation, demonstrates the necessity of the valuation of railroad property as an indispensable basis for securing to the people of this country just and reasonable rates. Before this bill becomes a law I trust that the amendment which I shall offer, or some better one, will be incorporated, making full and complete provision at an early date for the true valuation of all the railroad property of the United States.

I can not refrain from suggesting, Mr. President, that the railroads of this country can no longer afford to oppose this valuation. It is best for them that it should be known. They contend that their railroads are worth the amount for which they are capitalized. The public contends that the capitalization is grossly in excess of the fair value and not a lawful basis for taxing transportation. This great issue between the public and the railroads can be juggled with no longer. It can not be settled by legislation which palliates the wrong. It must be settled by getting the true value, the fair value of railway property. If there is to be an end of antagonism and dissension between the people and the transportation companies, it can be found, sir, in no other way.

8

La Follette Makes the Senators Put Their Votes on the Record

Just before the Senate finally voted on the Hepburn bill, Senator La Follette summed up his dissatisfaction with its weaknesses and recounted the failure of his attempts to strengthen it. He was to later campaign against Republican senators who had voted against his proposed amendments.

Document†

Mr. LA FOLLETTE. Mr. President, before I record my vote on this bill I desire to enter both a denial and a protest.

I deny that this bill complies with the recommendations of the President. I protest against every attempt to make it a partisan measure.

The President, in his message in 1901, urged upon Congress the amendment of the interstate-commerce act, declaring in that message that the people of this country were entitled to "just rates." In 1904 he recommended such legislation as would insure "reasonable rates." In 1905 he recommended such legislation as would insure "maximum reasonable rates."

This bill does not comply with any of the recommendations of the President. It will not enable the public to obtain the "just rates" recommended in 1901 or the reasonable rates recommended in 1904. It does not contain provisions that will enable the commission even to ascertain the "reasonable maximum rates" recommended in 1905.

I desire, sir, to protest against making this a political or partisan question. This has been attempted since this measure has been under consideration. The Senate may give it that appearance, but it can not be made a partisan issue before the country. This Senate, under the lead of certain Republican Senators, may seek to draw party lines, but they will fail when they carry the question back to the people in the States. You can not divide the people of this country on political lines upon a question as to whether the public-service corporations of the country shall serve the people of the country fairly, equitably, reasonably, justly.

†From: U.S., Senate, *Congressional Record*, 59th Cong., 1st sess., 1906, vol. 40, pt. 8, pp. 7083-84.

I offered several amendments to this bill. I offered no amendment upon which any political question ought to have been raised or any party vote cast. Every amendment which I offered would have strengthened its provisions and made it more just to the shippers, the consumers, and yet not one of those amendments was unfair to the carriers of this country.

I proposed the following amendments to this bill:

1. To restore the penalty of imprisonment for violations of the interstate-commerce law.

This amendment was defeated by a vote of 49 noes to 27 ayes. Forty-seven of the negative votes being those of Republican and two of Democratic Senators; of the votes for the amendment, twenty-six of the Senators voting were Democrats.

2. To strike out the two-year limitation, by the terms of which orders of the Commission expire two years from the time when such orders go into effect.

This amendment was rejected without a roll call, the votes in opposition thereto coming from Republican Senators.

3. To provide that when testimony is offered upon trial different from the testimony upon which the order of the Commission is based, testimony shall be taken by the trial court, the action suspended for fifteen days, the evidence certified back to the Commission, and the Commission given an opportunity to modify or revoke its former order.

This amendment was defeated—ayes 26, noes 49. Twenty-five Democratic Senators voted for the amendment; forty-eight Republican Senators voted against the amendment.

4. Substitute to section 15 providing for—

(a) Authority for the Commission to issue orders upon its own motion.

(b) To fix a maximum rate.

(c) To fix a differential, and to prescribe both a maximum and a minimum rate.

(d) To change the classification of any article.

(e) To determine what regulation or practice in respect to transportation is just and reasonable.

All Republican Senators who voted, excepting myself, voting against the amendment.

5. To forbid every Federal judge who owns shares of stock or bonds of a common carrier subject to the provisions of this act, or who uses a free pass or procures for the use of others free passes over such railroads, from hearing or deciding any proceeding or presiding at any trial under the provisions of this act.

Laid upon the table by a vote of 40 to 27—forty Republican Senators voting in the affirmative, twenty-five Democratic Senators voting in the negative.

6. That upon the trial of any action brought to set aside or modify any order made by the Commission a copy of the evidence introduced by the

plaintiff shall, upon motion made on behalf of the Commission, be transmitted to the Commission, and the court shall stay further proceedings in such action for fifteen days from the date of such transmission that the Commission upon receipt of such evidence may alter, modify, or amend the same. The amended order shall take the place of the original order, as though made by the Commission in the first instance.

The amendment was laid upon the table without debate—ayes 41, noes 30. Forty Republican Senators voted to lay the motion on the table. All Senators voting in the negative were Democrats excepting four.

7. That the Commission shall estimate and ascertain the fair value of the property of every railroad engaged in interstate commerce, as defined in this act, and used by it for the convenience of the public.

Motion to lay on the table rejected by a viva voce vote. Motion later renewed, and amendment laid on the table—ayes 40, noes 27. Thirty-nine Republican Senators voted to lay the amendment on the table. All votes against laying the amendment on the table were recorded by Democratic Senators excepting six.

8. To adopt the block system, insuring greater safety to the traveling public. Amendment rejected without roll call. All votes against the amendment coming from the Republican side of the Chamber.

9. For the railway employers' liability amendment for the relief of railway employees.

Defeated—ayes 28, noes 45. Those who voted in the affirmative were all Democrats excepting four. Of those voting against the amendment all were Republicans excepting three.

There can not be offered here or before the country any satisfactory argument or reason against the amendments which I proposed. No arguments have been made or reasons offered against their adoption. My Republican colleagues, under the leadership of a few New England Senators, lined up to vote down those amendments in nearly every instance without explanation or justification.

This bill, when it becomes a law, will not put this question at rest. It can not. When Congress merely clothes the Commission with power to ascertain whether rates are relatively equal and withholds from it all authority and all means of determining whether those rates are just and reasonable, it can not be expected that such inadequate legislation will solve this great problem and satisfy the public demand for not only equal but also just and reasonable rates.

The question which this bill should settle, but does not settle, will be a live issue in the next campaign for the election of men to both branches of Congress who will stand for a full measure of relief from oppressive transportation abuses.

So long as the legislation relative to the common carriers of this country permits these corporations to increase their capital stock without limit, increase it without adding anything of value to their properties, and increase it solely with the purpose of fixing rates upon that inflated capitalization, in order to pay profits and dividends to those holding the stocks and bonds, in which they have no real investment, just so long this question will be a vital issue before the American people.

There is to-day in the stock and bond valuation of the railroads of this country upward of seven billions of water. If the American people are expected to continue to pay transportation charges that will make a return upon that valuation, the temper of the people of this country is not understood here. Until there is invested in this Commission or some other authoritative body the power to determine the real, true valuation of the railroads of this country and the authority to fix rates so that they shall bear only a fair return upon that fair value, Senators may as well understand now that you will have this question constantly before you. It will not be possible to suppress it or keep it within the closed doors of committees for nine years to come. At every session, until an adequate measure is adopted, while I remain a member of this body the demand will be made here for legislation that will insure to the people of every State fair treatment at the hands of the common carriers of the country.

9

Senator Newlands for Stronger Railroad Regulation

Democratic Senator Newlands wanted Congress to provide for a more efficient national railroad system, by permitting consolidation and giving all regulatory and tax responsibility to the national government. In speeches and articles, he set forth the benefits of his plan.

Document†

Common Sense of the Railroad Question

.... I cannot agree with the railroad operators that nothing should be done. The power to fix rates of transportation is the power to affect the cost of everything which enters into common consumption, and, thus, in great measure, to regulate the standard of living of our people. Such tremendous power cannot safely be left, without restraint, in private hands.

As to the measure which passed the House by the overwhelming vote of 326 to 17, I fear it will be disappointing in its results. It does not present a scientific solution of the problem. It leaves the power of taxation with forty-five States and thousands of local political subdivisions, so that there can be nothing in the way of uniformity or permanency in this item. It makes no provision for the valuation of the property, nor does it make any attempt to indicate what would constitute a reasonable rate of interest on the investment. It does not touch the evil of overcapitalization, nor does it propose anything which would abate the alarming evil of political control which has come as an unavoidable incident in the growth of corporate power.

While the sentiment favoring Government ownership is increasing, it is plain that the country is not ready for such ownership at this time. The most serious objection to it is that it would interject 1,300,000 employees into the political patronage and render it difficult to drive from power the party controlling this vast influence, however desirable a change of administration might be.

†From: *The North American Review*, vol. 180 (1905), pp. 576-85.

On January 4th, I introduced a joint resolution in the Senate (S.R. 86, 59th Cong., 3d Sess.) providing for the appointment of a special commission, to consist of four experts on transportation and transportation law, five Senators and five Representatives, instructed to frame and report to Congress a national incorporation act. . . .

The object of my resolution is to unify and simplify the railroad administration of the country; to recognize the evolution in railroading, under which the operation and management of almost the entire railroad mileage has come under the control of about six well-known groups or systems; to place such systems under national incorporation and control; to make the taxes of the railroads fixed and certain; and to provide for fixed dividends, so that hereafter any increase of business will tend mathematically either to a betterment of the roads, to an increase in wages, or to a diminution in rates. These purposes I would accomplish by the following methods:

1. The requirement that all railroads engaging in interstate commerce shall incorporate under a national law in accordance with certain conditions not only permitting, but favoring, the consolidation of railroads.

2. The valuation of all such railroads by the Interstate Commerce Commission, and a capitalization not exceeding such valuation.

3. The revision by the Interstate Commerce Commission of all rates, so applied as to yield an annual return of not less than four per cent. on such valuation.

4. The exemption of railroad property, including stocks and bonds, from all taxes except a tax on gross receipts, such tax to begin at three per cent. and increase at the rate of one-fifth of one per cent. each year, until it reaches the maximum of five per cent. This tax to be collected by the Government, then distributed among the States and Territories on some equitable basis.

5. The creation of a pension fund for employees disqualified, either by injury or by age, from active service, by setting aside in the treasury a percentage of the gross receipts of the railroads.

6. The arbitration of all disputes between such railroad corporations and their employees as to compensation, hours of labor, and protection to life and limb.

In the United States, there are 200,000 miles of railroad, owned by about 2,000 corporations, and controlled by about 600 operating companies. But these operating companies have gradually come under the management of six great groups of ownership, each group dominated by a single individual, or by a few individuals. These groups are popularly known as "The Morgan," "The Gould-Rockefeller," "The Harriman," "The Vanderbilt," "The Pennsylvania" and "The Moore" groups. . . .

The fact is that the railroad, whether in the hands of the Government or of a private corporation, is a national monopoly. The steady trend of consolidation is the outcome of economic forces which cannot be controlled or appreciably impeded by legislation. The present system is complicated and expensive, involving the maintenance of many unnecessary corporations, the bond and stock issues of which constitute a mass of perplexity confusing alike to the investor, to the tax-assessor, and to the rate-regulating Commission. . . .

I would require all railroads engaged in interstate commerce to incorporate under a national law, and thus remove every barrier in the way of complete consolidation. I would provide that the amount of stocks and bonds issued for such consolidation should be approved by the Interstate Commerce Commission, and that they should not exceed the actual value of the railroads consolidated, such value to be determined by the Commission. I would provide that the Commission should approve the amount of bonds and stock to be issued for the purchase of connecting or intersecting lines, for the betterment of existing roads, and the construction of new ones; and I would make a rigid requirement to the effect that these securities should not exceed the value of the property acquired or the actual cost of the work constructed. This method would effectually prevent future overcapitalization. . . .

There is another advantage which would surely arise from the adoption of this policy, and which is of consequence equal to, if not greater than, the advantages which would follow fixed taxes and dividends and permanent peace for the railroad industry. This is the fact that the railroad would go out of politics. The railroad is in politics to-day because its vast property, amounting to more than ten billions, is between the upper and the nether millstone,—the upper milestone of the rate-regulating power, and the nether millstone of the taxing power. Between the two, save for the protection of the courts, these properties can be ground to destruction. The uncertainty and insecurity of their situation compels the railroads to go into politics. Hence, they take part in the election of every official whose duty is likely to trench in any degree upon the taxing and rate-regulating power. Doing everything systematically, their participation in politics means the organization of a machine in every State of the Union; and, since they pursue the lines of least resistance, this often means alliance with the corrupt element of every community. It is expensive for the railroads; and, worse than that, it is a grave menace to the institutions of the Republic.

I submit that these plans may reasonably be characterized as the common sense of the railroad question. Railroad monopoly has come in the course of natural evolution. We have learned that monopoly is inherent in our modern method of transportation. Let it be no longer outlawed, but frankly recognized, welcomed and made legal. The way to do this is by means of national incorporation.

Under this plan, the vast increase of transportation business in the future will tend to the reduction of rates and the advantage of the people. The appreciation of values which has occurred up to the time this act goes into effect rightfully belongs to the owners of railroad property. They invested in a speculative undertaking, took their chances, and created a property valuable to themselves and indispensable to the public. But now we propose to eliminate the speculative element, and to create conditions which will make railroad securities almost as good as Government bonds. In return for this great advantage, we ask that capital shall be content with a reasonable dividend upon *present* valuation. The increase in business which will inevitably arise in the future with the growth of the country will then inure to the benefit of the people in three forms. First, they will get it in the form of betterments, extensions, and constantly improving service. They will get it in the form of better conditions of employment—higher wages and shorter hours for the 1,300,000 men actually engaged in the railroad industry, and a pension fund to secure them in sickness or old age. Finally, this increase will be transmuted into public benefits, in the form of constantly lowering rates of freight and passenger traffic. . . .

While this joint resolution does not pretend to be a perfected piece of legislation, I believe it contains the germ of a railroad policy which will do equal and exact justice to all parties concerned. To capital, it will give security and assured dividends; to labor, it will give an impartial tribunal for the arbitration of disputes as to wages, hours and safety appliances; to the public, the lowest rates consistent with the investment and that high degree of efficiency which is born of modern methods. And to the capital invested, labor employed and the public served, it will, through the action of an impartial tribunal of high character and dignity, charged with the duty of settling all disputes, bring peace and immunity from constant agitation, and put an end to the continuous warfare which has heretofore existed between the railroad and its employees, and the railroad and the public.

It is plain enough that the people are restive under existing conditions. They are alarmed by the evidence that railroad rates are likely to fall under the absolute control of a few men, and that individuals will be subject to the absolute sway of these few men in matters vitally affecting their interests. The railroads are public highways. The service is a public service, and the conviction is gradually growing in favor of Government ownership.

Unless the railroad system is unified and simplified, the complexity of the situation will drive the country to Government ownership as a solution of the difficulty. . . .

The plan of Government ownership has the attractiveness of simplicity and directness. National ownership can, in my judgment, be met successfully only by a policy of national incorporation and control, which has the advantage of almost equal simplicity and directness. I believe the policy I am advocating would give the country nearly all the benefits of Government ownership, with none of its dangers. It would abolish the evils arising from unrestricted monopoly, prevent the entrance of over a million men into the political patronage, eliminate the present corporate interference with and control of our politics and retain in the transportation service the initiative, the enterprise and the administrative capacity of the brilliant men whose genius created our present magnificent system of transportation out of the crude conditions which prevailed a generation ago.

FRANCIS G. NEWLANDS.

10

The Desirability of Public Ownership

Professor Frank Parsons of Boston University was probably the most active single advocate of public ownership of the railroads. In books, articles, and expert testimony, he pointed out the benefits of national ownership abroad and contrasted it with railroad corruption and problems in America.

Document†

I believe that the public system favors the development of high character and intelligence among the people to a greater extent than the private system, and thereby every step toward public ownership through these effects, and by eliminating conflict and mastery between man and man, developing sympathy, and giving labor fuller opportunities for education and development, tends to secure the very conditions of a further rational and practical advance into the field of public ownership, so the advance of public ownership is the cure of the conditions which make public ownership difficult. It is its own road builder, step by step. It does not come all at once; it is a growth like the life of a youth, each year preparing him for the fuller and more arduous life of the years to come.

Under the public system, therefore, summing up the points I have tried to make, civilization, as a whole, appears to me to be favored as to mobility, as to moral development, as to political purification, as to treatment of employees, as to coordination of industry, as to application of the cooperative principle, as to justice in the administration and making of rates, as to aim and the whole tendency of the system toward a public instead of a private purpose, every test of civilization points to a system of public operation of public utilities as the ideal.

As a consequence of such a system our science of society will become a unified whole instead of a severed system, as it is now. The old political economy is like the old astronomy. The old astronomy thought the world was stationary at the center of the universe, and looked at the stars and sun as things going round the earth; and the old political economy thought that material wealth was the center of all things human. The new astronomy knows that the earth is not the center, and stands off and looks at the world

†From: U.S., Congress, House, *Industrial Commission Reports,* 57th Cong., 1st sess., 1902, House Document No. 178, vol. 9, pp. 167-68, 170-72.

and gets its true relation to the sun and the stars and the moon; and the new economy knows that material wealth is not the real center of human life; it stands off and looks at it and gets its true relations to mind, soul, affections, government, ideals, and human development. The importance of this is apparent when we note that if your government says, "Democracy, power in the people," and your industry says, "Aristocracy, plutocracy, power in the few"; if your jurisprudence says "Justice," and your economy says, "Get rich"; if your ethics and your religion say, "Love, service, devotion," and your economy says, "Self-interest, conquest, mastery," there is civil war in your social science; and we can not have a unified, consistent body of thought and principles until we get rid of these contradictions, and coordinate our political economy, our government, and our jurisprudence with ethics, and make them all one harmonious system under the law of love and service.

(The commission took a recess till 10:45 a.m., January 5, 1901, at which time Mr. Parsons continued his testimony, as follows:)

The Growth of Public Ownership

The WITNESS. The next point in order in my thought is the growth of public ownership and the development of sentiment in favor of it. I have already spoken to some extent of the development of public ownership of railways and of the fact that the two systems were tried in Belgium and Prussia, and Austria-Hungary, side by side, with results favorable to the public railways. I did not speak of the experience of Australasia. There they started with private systems, as they did also in Prussia, and they had the same experience that private systems were unsatisfactory, and have changed now in all the colonies of Australia and in New Zealand, so that almost the whole system is under public management. The South African Republics have State railroads, the Orange Free State taking the roads over in 1897. Cape Colony owns 2,000 out of 2,350 miles, and Natal owns all. So we find under all sorts of government—monarchical, constitutional, republican, or democratic to the last degree, as in New Zealand—this same tendency of the railroad system to be absorbed by the Government.

When we come to the telegraph and telephone the same thing is apparent. England tried the private telegraph system for over a quarter of a century, and after investigating fully the systems of public telegraph in other countries, decided to make her system public, and has tried that for 30 years with great success and with acknowledged superiority to the former private plan in the same country. With the telephone the French Government tried private concessions first, and finding the private operation unsatisfactory, took the telephones over and made them a public institution. England has followed the same path, making the telephone private first, and now it has taken over the trunk lines and is proceeding to absorb the exchanges. In Australasia—in some of the colonies—the first telephones were private, as in Victoria, and again the private system proved unsatisfactory, and the government decided to make the service public. Those are just a few illustrations from many.

If we look at waterworks and electric-light plants in our own country we find the movement very strong in the direction of public ownership. The number of public electric-light plants in the United States has risen from 1 to 1880 to about 400 now, while public water systems have increased from 1 in 16 in 1800 to 1,690 in 3,179 in 1896, or from about 6 per cent to about 53 per cent of the total. Of the 50 largest cities in the United States, 21 originally built and now own their waterworks, 20 have changed from private to public ownership, only 9 being now dependent on private companies for their supplies, and several of the 9 are considering a change to the public system. Fifty years ago the idea of public ownership of waterworks was vigorously combated and objections urged very similar to those now raised against public ownership of street railways and railroads. But in Massachusetts now 75 per cent of the waterworks are public; in Illinois, 78 per cent; Michigan, 81 per cent; Iowa, 82 per cent; Minnesota, 87 percent; Nebraska, 88 per cent, etc., and public water supply is quite universally recognized to be the proper thing. Another half century will probably see as great a change in sentiment and practice in the field of transportation.

... Stating briefly the difficulties with private railways already spoken of and some others not yet mentioned, and placing in a parallel column the advantages of national ownership of railways, we have the following summary:

Difficulties with private railways

1. Wrong aim: Private profit in place of the public good, dollars and cents instead of social service, dividends for a few instead of benefit for all, mastery and money instead of partnership and manhood.

2. Antagonism of interest between the owners and the public.

3. Lack of due coordination or else a consolidation too vast and powerful to be safe in private hands; a giant monopoly overriding and defying the regulative power of government.

4. An economic waste of hundreds of millions a year.

5. Watered stock and inflated capital, about half the capitalization of our railroads being fictitious, according to Poor and other high authorities.

6. No effort to free transportation from capital charges by the progressive cancellation of bonded or other indebtedness, but, on the contrary, a progressive piling up of capital without even the writing off of depreciation. As to the stock capital, a private road could not be expected to clear that off, since the owners can not be expected to give the road to the public as a present.

7. Higher charges than need be; an effort to obtain all the traffic will bear.

8. Fluctuating and chaotic rates favoring speculation, but throwing honest prevision off its hinges.

9. Unjust discrimination between persons, places, and industries. Free passes, secret rebates, differential preferences, etc.

10. Excessive reduction of rates at competitive points and overcharges on local traffic, to the injury of country districts and the overrapid growth of the cities.

11. No effort to relieve the pressure in the tenement districts of the great cities.

12. Defiance of law when it interferes with powerful railroad interests.

13. Purchase of legislation when practicable and useful to railroad interests.

14. Building and sustaining other monopolies and trusts, by privileges that enable them to control the markets.

15. Creating millionaires and disturbing the fair distribution of wealth.

16. A cause, at times, of industrial disturbance and depression and even panic.

17. Gambling in railway stocks and manipulation of their value by seesawing traffic, withholding dividends, or paying unearned profits, etc.

18. Exorbitant salaries for managers, with long hours, low wages, black listing, and other unfair treatment for ordinary employees, and disturbance of industry by periodic strikes.

19. Insufficient regard to safety of employees, passengers, and the public.

20. Imperfect coordination with the military department in time of war.

21. Injury to political honesty and good government through railway lobbies and the corrupting pressure of enormous private interests.

22. Great opportunity for success by fraud and indirection. (Read Wealth against the Commonwealth.)

23. Moral debasement of business men and degradation of the ideals of youth, through the spectacle of enormous wealth and power secured by railway rebates, manipulations of stock, fraudulent issues, and dishonest political action under railway pressure.

24. The payment of public moneys and gift of public lands to build railroads to be owned by private corporations and managed for their profit. The land and money, for instance, bestowed on the Illinois Central was enough to build and equip the whole road and give the company a bonus of $2,000,000 besides.

25. Private railways mean sovereign power in private hands—not only the sovereign power of modifying or nullifying the tariffs on imports, but the sovereign power to regulate commerce between our cities and States, to determine the distribution of wealth, the success or failure of individuals, the growth of cities, the development of the country, the life or death of industries, the power to tax the people without representation and for private purposes.

Advantages of public railways

1. True aim: Service and the public interest first; financial gain subordinate to justice and social welfare.

2. Harmony of interest by making the owners and the public one and the same.

3. Full coordination with entire safety to the public, because the combination belongs to the public, and, with a few simple safeguards, is easily held to the public interest.

4. An economic saving of hundreds of millions a year.

5. No inflation of capital, but, on the contrary, an effort to get rid of the wind and water in the capital of purchased lines.

6. The progressive cancellation of the whole capital, so that transportation may be freed from the burden of interest and dividend charges.

7. Lower charges than private roads can make under the same conditions, and a definite policy of reducing rates as one of the leading objects of the administration.

8. Steady and uniform rates favoring honest prevision and cutting the ground from under speculation.

9. Fair and impartial treatment of individuals; no secret rebates, passes only to those who render an equivalent in public service; equal rights to places and industries under the broad principles of the zone tariff or other equitable system.

10. Due concessions to through traffic, but earnest attention also to the reduction of local rates to give the small towns and rural districts their fair share of the advantages of cheap transportation.

11. A wise use of the roads to relieve the pressure of population and secure a healthful distribution of the people.

12. Conformity to law; the railroads and the lawmaking power being in the same hands.

13. No motive or power in public railroads to purchase legislation.

14. An important means of controlling the organization of capital, by refusing transportation to objectionable combines, instead of giving them secret rebates.

15. A powerful means of securing a better diffusion of wealth.

16. A means of regulating industry, relieving depression, and avoiding panic.

17. Removal of railway-stock gambling and manipulation.

18. Moderate salaries for managers, and altogether better treatment of ordinary employees, higher wages, shorter hours, more good homes, better citizenship, more contented and efficient labor, no strikes.

19. Better provision for the safety of employees, passengers, and the public.

20. An added source of strength in time of war.

21. Removal of one of the greatest sources of political corruption without incurring new danger if reasonable precautions are taken in respect to civil-service rules and nonpartisan management.

22. No opportunities for private fortune by fraud if a proper system of accounting and auditing is established. (Read the History of State Railroads.)

23. Removal of one prolific and all-pervading influence tending to moral debasement and low ideals.

24. When public money and land is devoted to building a public road the road belongs to the people who pay for it and the profits go into the public treasury.

25. Public administration of railways means the retention of sovereign power in the hands of the Government, where it belongs; the "public control

of public highways;" the public performance of a "public function;" the due enforcement of the tariff; the national regulation of commerce; an added justice, peace, and safety to industry, and an escape from one form of taxation without representation.

11

TR Calls for Regulation

In his annual State of the Union message of 1905, President Roosevelt made railroad regulation his first priority and explained why.

Document†

It is in the interest of the best type of railroad man and the best type of shipper no less than of the public that there should be governmental supervision and regulation of these great business operations, for the same reason that it is in the interest of the corporation which wishes to treat its employees aright that there should be an effective employers' liability act, or an effective system of factory laws to prevent the abuse of women and children. All such legislation frees the corporation that wishes to do well from being driven into doing ill, in order to compete with its rival, which prefers to do ill. We desire to set up a moral standard. There can be no delusion more fatal to the nation, than the delusion that the standard of profits, of business prosperity, is sufficient in judging any business or political question—from rate legislation to municipal government. Business success, whether for the individual or for the nation, is a good thing only so far as it is accompanied by and develops a high standard of conduct—honor, integrity, civic courage. The kind of business prosperity that blunts that standard of honor, that puts an inordinate value on mere wealth, that makes a man ruthless and conscienceless in trade, and weak and cowardly in citizenship, is not a good thing at all, but a very bad thing for the nation. This government stands for manhood first and for business only as an adjunct of manhood.

The question of transportation lies at the root of all industrial success, and the revolution in transportation which has taken place during the last half-century has been the most important factor in the growth of the new industrial conditions. Most emphatically we do not wish to see the man of great talents refused the reward for his talents. Still less do we wish to see him penalized; but we do desire to see the system of railroad transportation so handled that the strong man shall be given no advantage over the weak man. We wish to insure as fair treatment for the small town as for the big city; for the small shipper as for the big shipper. In the old days the highway of commerce, whether by water or by a road on land, was open to all; it belonged to the public and the traffic along it was free. At present the railway is this highway, and we must do our best to see that it is kept open to all on

†From: *Theodore Roosevelt: State Papers as Governor And President, 1899-1909*, ed. Hermann Hagedorn (New York, 1926), vol. 15, pp. 280-82.

equal terms. Unlike the old highway it is a very difficult and complex thing to manage, and it is far better that it should be managed by private individuals than by the government. But it can only be so managed on condition that justice is done the public. It is because, in my judgment, public ownership of railroads is highly undesirable and would probably in this country entail far-reaching disaster, that I wish to see such supervision and regulation of them in the interest of the public as will make it evident that there is no need for public ownership. The opponents of government regulation dwell upon the difficulties to be encountered and the intricate and involved nature of the problem. Their contention is true. It is a complicated and delicate problem, and all kinds of difficulties are sure to arise in connection with any plan of solution, while no plan will bring all the benefits hoped for by its more optimistic adherents. Moreover, under any healthy plan the benefits will develop gradually and not rapidly. Finally, we must clearly understand that the public servants who are to do this peculiarly responsible and delicate work must themselves be of the highest type both as regards integrity and efficiency. They must be well paid, for otherwise able men cannot in the long run be secured; and they must possess a lofty probity which will revolt as quickly at the thought of pandering to any gust of popular prejudice against rich men as at the thought of anything even remotely resembling subserviency to rich men. But while I fully admit the difficulties in the way, I do not for a moment admit that these difficulties warrant us in stopping in our effort to secure a wise and just system. They should have no other effect than to spur us on to the exercise of the resolution, the even-handed justice, and the fertility of resource, which we like to think of as typically American, and which will in the end achieve good results in this as in other fields of activity. The task is a great one and underlies the task of dealing with the whole industrial problem. But the fact that it is a great problem does not warrant us in shrinking from the attempt to solve it. At present we face such utter lack of supervision, such freedom from the restraints of law, that excellent men have often been literally forced into doing what they deplored because otherwise they were left at the mercy of unscrupulous competitors. To rail at and assail the men who have done as they best could under such conditions accomplishes little. What we need to do is to develop an orderly system, and such a system can only come through the gradually increased exercise of the right of efficient government control.

12

Justice To and From the Railroads

In a letter to the "muckraker" Ray Stannard Baker, President Roosevelt attacked both the railroad leaders and many of their critics and would-be regulators. He stated his belief that his "maximum rate" bill was all that could be pushed through Congress at that time, and advocated an experimental try-it-and-see policy.

Document†
TO RAY STANNARD BAKER
Personal

My dear Mr. Baker: I have your letter enclosing advance proof of your article. I think you are entirely mistaken in your depreciation of what is accomplished by fixing a maximum rate. Surely you must see that if the Commission has the power to make the maximum rate that which the railroad gives to the most favored shipper, it will speedily become impossible thus to favor any shipper save in altogether exceptional cases. I have gone all over the question of allowing the Commission to condemn the rate instead of fixing it, and am convinced that there is nothing in it. The railroads would eagerly accept such a proposition, because it would really leave the situation untouched. They would put in a new rate differing hardly at all from the old one. Fixing a maximum rate will not do all that is desired; but the power merely to condemn a rate and not to say what rate shall go into effect in its place would, I think, be a sham. I do not think it would accomplish any of the things that we wish. I shall go over your letter with Mr. Moody.

Do remember that while it is above all important to keep in mind the fact that there can be a substantial alleviation of almost every evil, it is of only secondary importance to keep in mind the further fact that no given measure and no given set of measures will work a perfect cure for any serious evil; and the insistence upon having only the perfect cure often results in securing no betterment whatever. I have had a great deal to do with railroads in the West, and a great deal to do with eastern legislatures which were dealing with railroads. I have often been impressed by the swinish indifference to right by certain railroad men in dealing both with the people and with railroads; but I am bound in honor to say that I have seen ten such exhibitions of indifference to the rights of railroads among legislatures and even among communities for one

†From: Roosevelt to Baker, November 20, 1905, in *The Letters of Theodore Roosevelt*, ed. Elting Morison (Cambridge, 1952), vol. 5, pp. 83-85, letter no. 3732.

that I have seen among the railroad people themselves. This is doubtless in part due to the fact that there are a great many more people who are not railroad kings than there are people who are railroad kings; but the fact remains that if you would examine the bills introduced in the New York legislature, for instance, about corporations, you would see that there are ten so-called strike bills—blackmail bills, ten bills improperly attacking railroads—for one bill to the improper advantage of railroads, or for one bill against their interests which ought to pass and of which they secure the defeat. Now, no dealing with the railroad problem is going to accomplish anything permanent unless as its main feature it contains insistence upon the fact that the first essential is honesty, and that the public conscience which regards with amused tolerance or approval a blackmailing attempt upon a railroad prepares the way for that railroad itself, by improper methods, getting something it ought not to have at some other time. Moreover, remember that if the management of the railroads was literally ideal there would remain an immense volume of complaint from individuals and localities; some of these complaints being due to simple ignorance, some to the fact that those who are foredoomed to failure like to cast the blame for their failure upon others.

So much for legislatures; now for the people at large. I have lived—not merely sojourned in, but lived—in Western communities where there were not railroads. Until railroads are built there is nothing the community will not promise in order to get them in; and I regret to state that after the railroad has come in the whole community is only too apt to pay attention to the demagogue who tries under one form or another to get them to repudiate their solemn promises to the railroad. They often promise too much; and they often fail to perform anything. Any movement conducted not on the ground of insisting upon justice *to* the railroads as well as *from* the railroads—any movement which limits itself simply to an attack upon railroads or upon the big corporations, is necessarily carried on in a spirit which invites disaster.

The railroads have been crazy in their hostility to my maximum rate proposition, and evidently do not share in the least your belief that nothing will result from it. I think that their alarm is foolishly overdrawn; and I have not a question that if we get the legislation there will be bitter disappointment among the people who expect, and have been taught to expect, the impossible. That it will accomplish some good I am certain. Moreover, it gives us a definite point of leverage. A single year's experience by the Commission in the enforcement of the maximum rate will show whether or not it fails in its purpose, as you anticipate that it will. If it makes such complete failure I do not believe there will be difficulty in at least trying the experiment in some shape or other of the definite rate. Meanwhile, I am absolutely certain that to adopt your proposal to substitute the power to condemn a rate for what we propose to do, would give not one particle of relief of any kind. I would not regard it as a bad power; I would simply regard it as a wholly ineffective power. I think it probably exists already; but if anyone wants to embody it in the bill, I have not the slightest objection, provided it is put in a separate paragraph so that there is no chance of its destroying the effect of the bill. I do not think it would accomplish any harm. I think it would merely accomplish nothing. *Sincerely yours*

13

Against the "Folly" of the Rich and the "Unhealthy" Excitement in the Public Mind

In a letter marked "confidential" and sent to his close friend and principal lieutenant, William Howard Taft, Roosevelt expressed his alarm over the popular unrest created by the greed of the rich and by the sensationalistic attacks on them in the magazines. To Taft, Roosevelt expounded his political philosophy of "conservatism and order" through constructive change.

Document†

. . . . I do not at all like the social conditions at present. The dull, purblind folly of the very rich men; their greed and arrogance, and the way in which they have unduly prospered by the help of the ablest lawyers, and too often through the weakness or shortsightedness of the judges or by their unfortunate possession of meticulous minds; these facts, and the corruption in business and politics, have tended to produce a very unhealthy condition of excitement and irritation in the popular mind, which shows itself in part in the enormous increase in the socialistic propaganda. Nothing effective, because nothing at once honest and intelligent, is being done to combat the great amount of evil which, mixed with a little good, a little truth, is contained in the outpourings of the *Cosmopolitan*, of *McClure's*, of *Collier's*, of Tom Lawson, David Graham Phillips of Upton Sinclair. Some of these are socialists; some of them merely lurid sensationalists; but they are all building up a revoluntary feeling which will most probably take the form of a political campaign. Then we may have to do, too late or almost too late, what had to be done in the silver campaign when in one summer we had to convince a great many good people that what they had been laboriously taught for several years previous was untrue. In the free silver campaign one most unhealthy feature of the situation was that in their panic the conservative forces selected as their real champion Hanna, a man with many good qualities, but who embodied in himself more than any other big man, all the

†From: Roosevelt to Taft, March 15, 1906, in *The Letters of Theodore Roosevelt*, ed. Elting Morison (Cambridge, 1952), pp. 183-84, letter no. 3854.

forces of coarse corruption that had been so prominent in our industrial and political life; and the respectable people either gave to him or approved of the giving to him of a colossal bribery fund. As it happens, I think that in that campaign for the most part the funds were honestly used as a means of convincing people; but the obligations Hanna incurred and the way in which the fund was raised were most unfortunate. I earnestly hope that if any similar contest of a more important kind has to be waged in the future that the friends of conservatism and order will make their fight under different kinds of leaders and by different methods.

14

Dolliver: In Favor of the Hepburn Bill

Senator Dolliver helped draw up the bill and fought it through the Senate Commerce Committee. Although the Democrat Ben Tillman of South Carolina was formally in charge during the Senate floor debate, Dolliver carried the major responsibility of guiding the bill through. In this speech, Dolliver referred to an article in the *North American Review* by Richard Olney, who challenged the constitutionality of regulation. Dolliver reminded the Senate that twelve years before, as President Grover Cleveland's Attorney General, Olney had used the "commerce power" to break the Pullman Strike of 1894. Dolliver also referred to the antiregulation campaign which the railroads were subsidizing in the press.

Document†

.... If the people of the United States have something to learn about the nature and justification of a railway rate, the accomplished gentlemen who have been selected to manage our railway properties have also something to learn about their relations to the public policy of the United States. I confess a certain degree of surprise that, after all that has happened in the world, and especially in the English-speaking world, it should be necessary for anybody to restate the position of public-service corporations under the laws of the land; but when so adroit and learned a lawyer as Mr. Richard Olney, formerly Secretary of State, writes of the Government regulation of railways exactly as if the law were attempting an unwarranted interference with the sacredness of private property, and solumnly disputes the power of Congress to discharge the very duty which the Constitution expressly assigns to it, it is time for some one who does not have to unload a lot of railway securities in order to acquire the spiritual preparation needed for the task to dig up a few first principles, if only to exhibit them as a background to the educational campaign which has been going on in the United States.

I do not know what business Mr. Olney is in now, but as I perused the *North American Review* containing his ponderous essay on this subject, with its curious warning to Congress not to exercise its power for fear that the States, misled by its example, might be tempted to exercise theirs, and seriously attempting to prove that the correction of unreasonable railway rates is substantially the same thing as the Government ownership of railroads

†From: U.S., Congress, Senate, *Congressional Record*, 59th Cong., 1st sess., 1906, vol. 40, pt. 4, pp. 3196, 3203.

and equally in contravention of our fundamental law, I found it hard to believe that this is the same man who, when he was Attorney-General, searching that simple clause of the Constitution found power enough in it to send the Army across the borders of Illinois and over riotous city limits, against the protests of panic-stricken mayors and screaming governors, to keep the peace of the United States and to open the highways of interstate traffic to the American people. I do not know what has come over the spirit of the old Attorney-General, but he is certainly not as vigorous as he once was. It may be that in trying to protect the Constitution of the United States he has broken down his own, or may be he is suffering from the effects of the pamphlets which swarmed in the mails during the past summer. [Laughter.]

****

It has been said that I have been misled into a socialistic agitation now general in the country. I do not think so. I will tell you one thing, however, that I do believe. I believe that the time is at hand when those who desire to defend the law of property had better consult together to bring back the old institutions of society to a situation where it can be defended. I am enlisted for that fight. I have not a trace of socialistic spirit in my thinking. I do not look forward to government ownership of anything—government ownership of railroads or farms or banks or any of the instrumentalities of commerce. I do not wish to see the Government doing the business of the American people and all the rest of us standing around in front of the gilded domes of our State capitols or our National Capitol waiting for our occasional dividend out of the gross product of nothing in particular. [Laughter.] I do not yield to the fascinations of that cheap philosophy of human life. I believe in the laws that have built society up on its present basis, and I will say to you gentlemen, especially those of you who are so concerned about the great interests of property in the United States, that a storm is gathering, and the time is approaching when the American people are going to make an inquiry into the methods by which men in a few years acquire hundreds of millions of dollars and rise to an influence that threatens to subordinate even the Government of the United States.

That inquiry will be made. When that time comes, I will be on hand to defend the law of property. Capital is the earnings and the savings of labor. I believe in that. Whoever charges me with trying to forward any scheme for government ownership of railroads, or any other socialistic experiment in the United States, misunderstands both my public record and my purpose as a humble worker in the ranks of our common citizenship.

I will say another thing. This same charge of socialism was made in England in the House of Commons when the Government undertook the same sort of management of railway properties that we contemplate here to-day. A man, whose name I can not recollect just now, a solid old Welshman, I think, got up in the House of Commons and said that instead of looking toward the government ownership of railroads, the people were taking the only possible step that could be taken to make the government ownership of railways impossible, at least for generations, in the United

Kingdom. I say now and here that unless we can in some way agree upon an effective regulation of railway rates we are face to face in America with problems which may ultimately involve a serious harm to our institutions by the forced resort of the people to untried methods in our business organization. I do not want to see that day, but I think I see far enough into the movements of public opinion to understand that unless the people of the United States are given some adequate protection against the abuses of railway management, or the possibility of such abuses arising in the future, there will be a formidable movement very much before the end of this generation in favor, heart and soul, of the governmental assumption of these great instrumentalities of commerce and of business.

15

Shortcomings of Regulatory Agencies

By the 1970s, as the economy was beset by simultaneous inflation and depression, both consumer-oriented and business-oriented critics placed great blame on the regulatory commissions. The regulators were accused of inhibiting competition and increasing costs through delay and incompetence.

Document†

How to Regulate the Regulators

What an absurd idea—a guardian to need a guardian!
—Plato's *Republic*

Gerald Ford, presiding over a republic somewhat less ideal than Plato's, disagrees. Last week, as part of his war on inflation, he urged the creation of a "National Commission on Regulatory Reform" that could indeed act as guardian of the guardians—the deeply entrenched, highly independent federal agencies that regulate everything from the air waves to pipelines. The commission's task will be formidable: to identify and eliminate the hodgepodge of antiquated rules that in Ford's words, "increase costs to the consumer without good reason in today's economic climate."

Such a housecleaning is long overdue. Beginning with the establishment of the Interstate Commerce Commission (ICC) by Congress 87 years ago to bring the freewheeling railroad barons into line, the regulatory agencies have proliferated by the score into today's alphabet soup. In 1920, Congress set up the Federal Power Commission (FPC) to watch over the burgeoning hydroelectric industry; in 1934, the Federal Communications Commission (FCC) to monitor the new radio industry; in 1938, the Civil Aeronautics Board (CAB) to police the airlanes; in 1946, the Atomic Energy Commission (AEC). Yet for all the genuine needs and good intentions of the time that brought them into being, the commissions have often become barnacled over the years. At times they seem more concerned with the interests of their industries than those of the public: rigging rates to protect even the most inefficient operators, discouraging new participants in a field and, worst of all, keeping consumer prices unnaturally high.

The excesses are acknowledged by many of the regulators themselves. In a speech in Detroit last week, Federal Trade Commission Chairman Lewis Engman, 38, a Nixon appointee, sounded almost like an echo of Consumerist

†From: *Time*, October 21, 1974, p. 58. Reprinted by permission from TIME, The Weekly Newsmagazine; Copyright Time Inc.

Ralph Nader, whose Center for the Study of Responsive Law has just published a massive 950-page citizens' guidebook to the "bureaucratic labyrinths" of the federal regulatory system. Said Engman: "Most regulated industries have become federal protectorates, living in a cozy world of cost-plus, safely protected from the ugly specters of competition, efficiency and innovation." Estimating that such protection adds $16 billion a year to the nation's transportation bill alone, Engman added: "Our system of hidden regulatory subsidies makes welfare fraud look like petty larceny."

Engman's charge does not, of course, apply across the board. Many federal agencies have performed with distinction in the public interest despite small staffs, low salaries and ever-present political pressures. Yet others have all too often been what Economist John Kenneth Galbraith calls "an arm of the industry they are regulating—or senile." To critics like Galbraith and Engman, the ICC in particular meets both disability tests. Although it has some 17,000 companies under its supervision—railroads, truckers, pipeline operators—it acts more like a mother hen than a watchdog. Trucks, for instance, are allowed to return home empty from deliveries (a rule, food retailers insist, that costs them $250 million in added freight each year. In turn, though railroads complain that the ICC favors truckers, they have been allowed to reduce or drop unprofitable passenger trains even when commuters need such service.

The agencies often defend such practices on the grounds that it serves the national interest to protect key industries—for example, faltering flag carriers like Pan American World Airways. Even so, such protective policies can backfire. They can encourage inefficiency; they can block badly needed new technologies. Communications satellites were long needed to relieve the overloaded U.S. long-distance telephone network, but largely because of FCC dawdling, the first domestic communications satellite was not launched until this year. By keeping natural-gas prices unreasonably low during the 1960s, the FPC discouraged exploration for new supplies and thereby helped create today's severe natural-gas shortage. (Paradoxically, after years of excessive regulation, the FPC now wants to stop gas regulation entirely, which prompts former FPC member Lee White to pose an intriguing question: Is it proper for a regulatory agency to deregulate itself?) Finally, some agencies may simply be redundant. An independent arm of the Treasury, the Comptroller of the Currency performs some of the same bank supervisory functions as the Federal Reserve and the Federal Deposit Insurance Corporation, and sometimes not as well: in a recent audit of New York's Franklin National Bank, it failed completely to spot any signs of that institution's impending collapse.

Reforming the regulatory agencies will not be easy. Indeed, the very nature of their multiple roles is often contradictory. As Lawyer Newton Minow, the FCC's former gadfly chairman, puts it: "I don't think you can be a legislator on Monday, a policeman on Wednesday and a judge on Friday." Beyond that, the agencies are richly staffed with political appointees who are often alumni of the very industries that they are supposed to regulate; they also are frequently vulnerable to powerful industrialist lobbyists.

Despite such obstacles, the national commission requested by President Ford should take some needed first steps. For example, it could ensure greater agency independence by insisting that commissioners and high-ranking employees come from industries other than those they will be required to regulate, and be forbidden for a period of time to join those industries after they leave Government service. More important, it could set new regulatory standards that require agencies to consider the consequences of every action they take: Does it promote or impede competition? Does it serve the interest of only one company or the nation at large? Finally, the commission should promote a new public awareness of the functions and objectives of the regulatory agencies in the hope that an aware citizenry will not allow a repetition of past agency indifference or abuse. The President is surely right in his perception that unregulated regulators are a luxury that the U.S. can no longer afford.

16

What J. P. Morgan Did to the New England Railroads

The ICC report to Congress in 1914 detailed the kind of financial manipulation that continued to take place despite the Hepburn Law. Between 1903 and 1913, J.P. Morgan was building a railroad monopoly in New England. To do it, he increased the capitalization of New England's railroads from $93 million to $417 million.

Document†

Interstate Commerce Commission
IN RE FINANCIAL TRANSACTIONS OF THE NEW YORK, NEW HAVEN & HARTFORD RAILROAD COMPANY.
Report of the Commission to the Senate of the United States

By The Commission:

The Commission has the honor to submit the following report in compliance with the resolution of the Senate dated February 7, 1914:

SCOPE OF THE INVESTIGATION

In the former investigation, known as the *New England Investigation*, 27 I.C.C. 560, the Commission had access only to the books of accounts of The New York, New Haven & Hartford Railroad Company, The Consolidated Railway Company, The Connecticut Company, and The Rhode Island Company. No minute books, stock books, or correspondence files of these companies were obtained in their entirety, but only such reference to same was available as was specifically requested. The financial affairs of these companies constituted only one branch of this investigation. In the present proceeding the Commission has inquired into the financial affairs of the entire New Haven system.

Since the former investigation there has been a change in the executive officers of the New Haven system. In justice to the present management it is but fair to say that its chief executive officer and his special counsel have

†From: U.S., Congress, Senate, *Report on Financial Transactions of New York, New Haven & Hartford Railroad*, 63rd Cong., 2nd sess., 1914, Senate Document No. 543, vol. 1, pp. 1-2.

cooperated with the Commission and rendered it substantial assistance throughout this investigation.

Public hearings were held extending over a period of 60 days of almost continuous session. Witnesses in a position to have knowledge of the transactions under scrutiny were examined. In the search for truth the Commission had to overcome many obstacles, such as the burning of books, letters, and documents and the obstinacy of witnesses who declined to testify until criminal proceedings were begun for their refusal to answer questions. The New Haven system has more than 300 subsidiary corporations, in a web of entangling alliances with each other, many of which were seemingly planned, created, and manipulated by lawyers expressly retained for the purpose of concealment or deception. Ordinarily in investigations of this character evidence is easily adduced by placing the witnesses upon the stand, but in this investigation the witnesses other than the accountants for the Commission were in the main hostile, and with few exceptions their testimony was unwillingly given. The result of our research into the financial workings of the former management of the New Haven system has been to disclose one of the most glaring instances of maladministration revealed in all the history of American railroading. In the course of the investigation many instances were uncovered of violation of the laws of different States. As these were not understood to be pertinent to our inquiry under the Senate resolution we did not follow them into their details. As pointing to violations of State laws, we have turned over the evidence concerning local occurrences in New York City to the district attorney for the proper district, and the testimony relating to irregularities in Massachusetts and Rhode Island have been laid before the proper authorities of those States. The Commission has also furnished the Department of Justice with a complete record of the testimony.

The difficulties under which this railroad system has labored in the past are internal and wholly due to its own mismanagement. Its troubles have not arisen because of regulation by governmental authority. Its greatest losses and most costly blunders were made in attempting to circumvent governmental regulation and to extend its domination beyond the limits fixed by law.

The subject matter of this inquiry relates to the financial operation of a railroad system which, on June 30, 1903, had a total capitalization of approximately $93,000,000, of which $79,000,000 was stock and $14,000,000 bonds. In the ten years from June 30, 1903, this capitalization was increased from $93,000,000 to $417,000,000, exclusive of stock premiums, or an increase of $324,000,000. Of this increase approximately $120,000,000 was devoted to its railroad property and was expended for betterments and equipment. This leaves the sum of $204,000,000, which was expended for operations outside of its railroad sphere. Through the expenditure of this sum this railroad system has practically monopolized the freight and passenger business in five of the States of the Union. It has acquired a monopoly of competing steamship lines and trolley systems in the section which it serves. The financial operations necessary for these acquisitions, and the losses which they have entailed, have been skillfully concealed by the juggling of money and securities from one subsidiary corporation to another.

17

The Bull Among the Cows

Peter Lyon, biographer of S.S. McClure, the man who "founded" muck-raking, has offered ironic comment on the meaning of J.P. Morgan's monopoly-building efforts in New England.

Document†

Morgan, who had been elected to the board of the New Haven in 1892, made Charles S. Mellen its president in 1903 just as he had previously made Mellen the president of the Northern Pacific. Later, when the Commission was investigating the collapse of the New Haven, the chief counsel asked Mellen:

Q: Were you Mr. Morgan's man as president of the New Haven?
A: I have been called his office-boy. I was very proud of his confidence.
I regard the statement that I was his man as a compliment.

The Morgan-Mellen regime lasted from 1903 to 1912 and was officially characterized as "one of the most glaring instances of maladministration in all the history of American railroading." Their aim was complete control of every type of public transportation in New England, or to it, or from it; and to encompass their aim the capitalization of the New Haven was increased from ninety-three million dollars in 1903 to four hundred and seventeen millions in 1912, mostly by issuing bonds, mostly to buy interurban trolley lines and steamship lines, mostly at grossly inflated prices, and always in the teeth of a blizzard of protests by businessmen, shippers, state legislators, investors, passengers, newspaper editors, and public-spirited citizens. One director made a profit of two million seven hundred thousand dollars simply for sequestering some shares of the Boston & Maine at a time when the purchase of that road by the New Haven was inconveniently illegal. Another road, the New York, Westchester & Boston, which was worth maybe twelve million dollars, was acquired by the New Haven for thirty-five million; the directors of the New Haven, who were given no idea of "what they were buying at such a big price," felt themselves obliged to inquire of President Mellen. Poor Mellen later testified as to what happened when he begged Morgan for some elucidation:

MELLEN: Can you give me a few moments?
MORGAN: Certainly.

†From: Peter Lyon, *To Hell In A Day Coach* (Philadelphia, 1968), pp. 134-36.

MELLEN: This note [for the purchase of the small railroad] is not in the form it should be—there should be additional information given.

MORGAN: Did not Mr. [Francis Lynde] Stetson draw that note?

MELLEN: Yes, I suppose so.

MORGAN: Do you think you know more how it ought to be done than he does?

After which Morgan wrathfully took up his stick and his hat and left.

For nine wretched years the story of the New Haven was one of reckless disregard of the public and of its investors, one of wholesale bribery, of corporate accounts falsified and unearned dividends declared, of dreadful accidents and unconscionable interruptions of service, of looting and corruption and financial chicanery. Mellen was once indicted for manslaughter and once for criminal restraint of trade. J.P. Morgan & Company were charged with having pocketed "excessive profits" in raising money for the road and were finally forced to withdraw as fiscal agents and to remove their representatives from the board of directors.

In 1914, when he was enduring one of several investigations by the Commission, Mellen grew pensive. "I think the record of the New Haven's transactions," he remarked, "with the elimination of Mr. Morgan, would have been as tame and uneventful, as devoid of interest and incident, as would the record of a herd of cows deprived of the association of a bull." Thus graphically, if unintentionally, Mellon suggested what Morgan did to the New Haven.

18

What Happened to the Penn Central

The Penn Central, the giant of the American rail systems, has been the victim of both adverse economic trends and mismanagement. As the railroad continued to lose money but remained an essential part of the transportation network, there was increasing talk of a quasi-socialist solution.

Document†

No one has invented a way for the United States to do without railroads, even if they fail financially. Without freight trains, the country's commerce would choke. The Penn Central, which carries more freight and loses more money than any enterprise in history, is surely the cutting edge of this capitalist dilemma. The map of the Penn Central system looks like a salamander, with its head in Boston, its tail in East St. Louis, and its four stubby legs running to Montreal, to the Delmarva Peninsula, to Northern Michigan and to West Virginia. Within the outlines of this huge animal, the network of Penn Central tracks forms a tight cross-hatched pattern, covering New York, Pennsylvania, Ohio and Indiana almost completely, as well as parts of 12 other states, two Canadian provinces and the District of Columbia. Penn Central, with 19,509 miles of railroad routes, would rank second in size to the Burlington Northern, if the criterion were total length. But as a freight mover, Penn Central is easily the biggest railroad in the country. Every day it carries 228,000 tons of coal, 65,000 tons of iron and other ores, 55,000 tons of food, 44,000 tons of pulp and paper and 24,000 tons of grain. In fact, in terms of freight-car miles, the Penn Central last year did the same amount of work that it would take to move a 35-car freight train to the sun.

Penn Central was until recent years the nation's largest passenger railroad, but by now it has moved out of the passenger business almost entirely, complaining that passenger trains don't make money. Its long-haul passenger business has been turned over to Amtrak, a Government-backed corporation, which operates its own trains over the tracks of Penn Central and other railroads and pays them for the use of their tracks and terminals. Penn Central still carries 225,000 commuters every day under full or partial subsidy arrangements with local government agencies, principally in Boston, Philadelphia and New York.

†From: Joseph Albright, "A hell of a way to run a government," *New York Times Magazine*, November 3, 1974, pp. 17, 94, 95.

Despite horrendous losses, the Penn Central Transportation Company remains a huge corporation, with $4-billion in assets, 78,000 employes and a multiplicity of interests. Last year, for instance, it laid 1,814,827 crossties. It also paid $2,128,000 to 24 law firms.

The Penn Central was acclaimed as the salvation of the Northeastern railroad system six years ago when it was formed in the merger of the cash-starved Pennsylvania, New York Central and New Haven railroads. The stock of the new Penn Central Transportation Company shot up to $86.50 a share within the first year, and soon Penn Central chairman Stuart Saunders, the main architect of the merger, was given a scroll as Businessman of the Year for 1968.

Two years later, during the recession of 1970, Penn Central crashed into bankruptcy and the stock dropped to $2 a share. The postmortems, which have gone on almost continually ever since, have tended to point in one of two directions. One school of thought explains the fiasco by pointing to the alleged misdeeds or misjudgements of the top executives, who hastily departed after the bankruptcy. One of the most eye-catching accusations, which emanated from a House subcommittee investigation, was that some Penn Central executives had siphoned off railroad revenues for an executive jet aviation subsidiary that provided call girls for customers. Lately, the Securities and Exchange Commission has charged Saunders and David C. Bevan, former Penn Central financial officer, with fraudulently scheming to inflate the company's reported earnings.

The other school of thought, more widely accepted in the railroad industry, but less publicized, is that Penn Central was the victim of broad economic trends in the Northeast. Factories that justified a rail spur 75 years ago have moved South, only to be replaced by service businesses and light industry. Coal, instead of being hauled to every factory, was now often being transformed into electricity near the mine head or not being mined at all. The interstate highway system and the St. Lawrence Seaway allowed trucks and barges to skim off the growth in freight tonnage. All this occurred in an industry historically burdened by hopelessly inefficient work rules won by unions over the years, and in an overdeveloped railroad environment. Intertwined with the Penn Central tracks, often duplicating them line for line, are those of eight other railroads, and since the Penn Central filed for bankruptcy, six of them have followed suit.

In retrospect, it is quite possible that both schools of thought are right about the Penn Central collapse. A more talented crew in the executive suites probably could have squeaked past bankruptcy court in 1970. On the other hand, the general railroad situation in the Northeast was out of phase with the economy of the nineteen-sixties, and it is valid to argue that the Penn Central would have lost money under any management. Indeed, since the court-appointed trustees took over from the Bevan-Saunders team, Penn Central, instead of prospering, has lost another $700-million. To keep from running out of cash to meet its payroll, the company's trustees have accepted $116-million in Government loans and loan guarantees and have postponed every possible debt or repair.

Reliance on such temporizing measures did nothing to prevent the roadbed and equipment from deteriorating, and before long the bankruptcy creditors were pressing in court for the liquidation of Penn Central and the cessation of its operations. It was to prevent this that Congress finally settled for the Shoup-Adams Act nearly a year ago. Under it, the freight-carrying system now belonging to Penn Central and four other smaller bankrupt railroads in the Northeast are supposed to be merged into a new federally assisted railroad corporation to be known as Consolidated Rail Corporation or Conrail for short. In exchange for their tracks, terminals locomotives and other rail properties, the creditors will get all the common stock in Conrail, plus something like $1-billion in Government-backed bonds.

Unless blocked by the Supreme Court, Conrail should begin operating the merged system—94 percent of which is now Penn Central—in 1976. Strictly speaking, the Government will not "own" its new creation, Conrail. But the new railroad will be Government-controlled at least until the midnineteen-eighties, and perhaps forever, because of a stipulation in the Shoup-Adams Act that the Conrail board of directors must be controlled by Government appointees as long as at least half of Conrail's outstanding loans are Government-assisted.

Conrail hopes to make a go of the Northeast rail system by spending Federal money on fixing up worn-out tracks and cars and, more important, by pruning to efficient size the "spaghetti" of duplicating and obsolete rail lines that helped drag not only the Penn Central but also the Erie Lackawanna, Boston & Main, Lehigh Valley, Ann Arbor, Reading, and Central of New Jersey into bankruptcy.

19

On How to Save the Railroads Without Nationalization

For more than a year, a government group commissioned by the Council of Economic Advisers and the National Commission on Productivity studied the railroad problem. In an article in the *Harvard Business Review*, the business school professors who headed the task force summed up its recommendations. Obviously working with a mandate to seek alternatives to nationalization, they suggested less "hampering" regulation, and called for the formation, under private control, of a series of transcontinental railroad systems. Under this proposal, the usual pattern of merging parallel railroads would be replaced by end-to-end mergers to produce nationwide railroads running from the Atlantic to the Pacific oceans and from the Gulf of Mexico to the Great Lakes.

Document†

Railroads, once the dominating demons of American big business, are clearly a sick industry. In 1973, our Class I railroads ranked 69th out of 70 major industrial groups in return on net worth (3%). And 1973 was a prosperous year; net railway operating income was 4% higher than in 1972 and 77% higher than in 1970.

Moreover, the situation is not restricted to the well-known difficulties of the northeastern railroads, six of which are in bankruptcy, or of several troubled granger (grain-hauling) roads teetering on the brink. Even the relatively prosperous southern roads have realized a rate of return on net investment in excess of 5% only twice in the last 18 years. During the same period the composite return of western lines has ranged between 2.4% and 4.2%.

The industry is even more sickly than these meager returns suggest. To preserve the appearance of profitability in lean years, managements have

†From: John R. Meyer and Alexander L. Morton, "A better way to run the railroads," *Harvard Business Review*, vol. 52 (July-August, 1974) pp. 141-8.

often postponed replacement of aging assets. These accumulated deferrals now threaten to bring large segments of the system to a halt. Some 40% of the Penn Central network is under "slow orders" restricting train speeds; nevertheless, the carrier had more than 600 derailments last January and more than 1,000 in February. . . .

Ten billion dollars, which exceeds total railway operating income for the last 15 years, is a conservative estimate of the cost to restore the nation's rail network to good operating standards.

Why do the rail carriers suffer such chronic ill health? There are many explanations, some going deep into the history of railroad development. One fundamental cause is adverse trends in traditional railroad markets. For example, with the emergence of autos and airplanes in intercity markets, rail passenger traffic has dwindled to a fraction of its former levels. Throughout the 50-year decline of passenger travel by rail (interrupted only during World War II), the railroads have found it difficult to cut back service as rapidly as traffic shrank. As a result, they have suffered operating losses on passenger service every year since 1930. Passenger deficits have averaged half a billion dollars since the end of World War II, eating up roughly one third to one half the operating profits which freight hauling generated.

Markets & Regulation

Freight traffic has sustained the industry. But because of the evolutionary path of the economy in the postwar period, the growth of freight traffic has slowed and the railroads' dominance of it has ended. As our economy shifts from one based on goods to one based on services, the tonnage of intercity freight moving by all modes has been growing only half as fast as real gross national product. Even in the manufacturing sector, change penalizes the railroads. Heavy manufacturing dominated U.S. business until the Depression. Now growth has been concentrated in light manufacturing industries that require little input of raw materials to make products of small weight in relation to their value. . . . Freight revenues now exceed rail freight revenues by five to one. The loss in railroad market share is due not only to ineffective competition against the newer modes, but also to the faster growth in types of freight for which other modes of traffic enjoy natural cost and service advantages. Pipelines are better suited for moving petroleum and petroleum products, while trucks have service (and sometimes cost) advantages for shipping small quantities of light, high-value manufactures in short, intra-metropolitan movements.

Regulation . . . circumscribes the freedom of railroad management to adapt operations to both evolving markets and intensifying competition. Regulation greatly encumbers rate making, a vital marketing tool. Inasmuch as technological innovations almost inevitably require collateral pricing innovations, regulation impedes technological progress as well. Regulatory procedures and decisions have outrageously delayed abandonment of services that no longer attract sufficient patronage to defray their costs—some light-density branch lines, passenger trains, and terminal switching. Mergers, provision of ancillary truck or barge services, financial decisions, and other basic responsibilities and normal prerogatives of corporate management have been subject to detailed regulatory scrutiny and, in many instances, to prohibitions.

Over the years the effect of pervasive regulation on the industry has extended beyond the mere blunting and distorting of management initiatives; it has influenced the quality of management. Some American railroads have been poorly run. To some extent, mismanagement is induced by what might be called the "regulatory syndrome"—a condition leading to more concern with meeting or circumventing legalities than with rendering better service at lower cost.

Government involvement in transportation has worked to the railroads' detriment in other respects too. Since 1921 the government has invested more than $350 billion in the highway network. Although it is debatable whether this expenditure has heavily subsidized trucking (since the bulk of the money has been raised by gasoline taxes and other user charges), it is inarguable that public highways have been a boon to trucking. Similarly, national defense outlays have greatly helped airline development; also, barges on inland waterways have not paid the full costs (often inflated by nontransportation considerations) of the federally financed improvements they use. In contrast, discriminatory property taxation by states and localities costs the railroads an estimated $70 million per year. While public investment in competitive modes of transportation has contributed to the railroads' difficulties, the fundamental problem has been and continues to be adapting to adverse market trends in a constrained and highly regulated environment.

More Productive Capital & Labor . . .

In recent years, railroad managements have pursued a variety of strategies to deal with their traffic losses and financial stringencies. Discontinuation of unprofitable services has been one. For example, annual losses from passenger service (mostly commuter) are now less than $100 million, compared with $400 million to $500 million in the 1960s. Railroads have also abandoned many light-volume branch lines, particularly in New England and the granger territory. Mainline segments of several systems, such as the Central of New Jersey and the Rutland, have been abandoned completely. In addition, some categories of freight business whose costs were thought to exceed revenues have been trimmed, such as moving less-than-carloads, providing various switching and terminal services, and transporting certain commodities like livestock and fresh produce.

The railroads have also sought a cure for substandard profits in their determined pursuit of technological innovation. In no other aspect of the industry has change been so dramatic. Larger freight cars of specialized design, "piggyback" operations, and unit trains are readily visible examples. Electronic signaling and train-control systems, automated classification yards, and computerization of many clerical functions have further helped to modernize railroading. . . .

Many merging roads, in order to achieve governmental approval of their plans, have also agreed to costly labor protection clauses. The Penn Central is a case in point. Regulation of service discontinuance and abandonment has hampered the elimination of parallel routes and duplicate facilities. Combined systems, by definition, are larger than their former parts, and the management problems thus created (and often exacerbated by the merger partners' different management styles) have often proved substantial. Sometimes it is tempting to conceive of a Gresham's law of railroading which asserts that bad managements "merge out" the good. . . .

For a more prosperous future, the railroads must improve rail service and expand traffic by developing new freight markets and recapturing business for which rails have inherent advantages. As a corollary, cost cutting should be deemphasized, though certainly not abandoned, and the emphasis put on gaining economies through better capital utilization rather than through labor force reduction. Better utilization of the car fleet, for example, could generate substantial capital savings.

Essentials for Better Service

In the long run, however, the key to a more successful railroad marketing strategy is faster, more regular and dependable, and damage-free service. With better service the railroads could recapture part of the large volume of long-haul traffic in manufactures that now move by truck, but for which rail carriers have potential cost (and possibly service) advantages. Such traffic, moreover, tends to have high profit margins. Four reforms are essential for achieving this marketing reorientation:

1

The industry should embrace the container as its basic method for moving high-value manufactured goods. The objective should be the creation of a modern, specialized fleet to replace the all-purpose boxcars. . . .

2

The industry should use shorter, more frequent freight trains and adopt more scientific management of the freight fleet. . . .

3

Government regulation of rates, types of service, and abandonments—in fact, regulation of all aspects of transportation management—should be eased. . . .

4

In what might be the most controversial and farreaching move, four to seven nationwide rail systems should be formed through a succession of predominantly end-to-end mergers (in contrast to the usual parallel mergers). Some of these systems would be truly transcontinantal—extending from the Atlantic to the Pacific—and some would be oriented toward a north-south axis—extending, say, from the Gulf of Mexico to the Great Lakes. But each would reach every major market in its area.

Perhaps the most significant benefit from this consolidation would be a vast reduction in "interlining," or traffic interchange among railroads. There are 38 independent "regional" railroad systems in the United States; roughly half of all rail shipments (accounting for 70% of revenue ton-miles) employ two or more of these lines to move from origin to destination. Switching expenses, clerical and administrative expenses, and delays make the process of transferring a shipment from one carrier to another very costly. In Chicago (probably the worst example), shipments typically take three days to move between eastern and western trunk lines.

Nationalization the Alternative?

Will these reforms—some new, some old—solve the railroad problem in this country? One can be hopeful but hardly certain. What *is* certain is that these policies would almost surely be superior to the major alternatives, most of which would probably end up in nationalization of a considerable part, if not all, of the present network.

Although nationalization can certainly solve immediate financial problems (mainly by easing operating losses through the Treasury), other countries have found that it almost invariably "politicizes" management decisions. This, in turn, creates and then makes effective an entrenched opposition to reform. Not surprisingly, therefore, deficits can mount faster *after* nationalization, making long-term structural reform even harder to achieve. As the Penn Central continues to slide deeper into the red and the cynics begin to outnumber the defenders of the federal plan to rescue the eastern bankrupts, it becomes ever clearer that new and bold steps must be taken if nationalization is to be denied.

part three

Bibliographic Essay

Despite the existence of general interest in railroading and numerous accounts of particular railroads, remarkably few broad histories have been written. Rixon Bucknall, *Trains* (New York, 1971) offers a fine, illustrated, popular introduction to everything about the subject. Paul Hastings, *Railroads, An International History* (New York, 1972) tells the story of railroads around the world. Michael Robbins, *The Railway Age in Britain* (London, 1962) is a scholarly account of the British experience and world impact.

General histories of the American railroads are also surprisingly scarce and almost all argumentative. John F. Stover, *American Railroads* (Chicago, 1961), is a well-balanced though admiring account. He has rewritten and extended the story in *The Life and Decline of the American Railroad* (New York, 1970), which is full of useful information and analysis but inclined to rapture about the achievements of railroad managers and technology. On the other hand, the book by Peter Lyon, grandson and biographer of the founder of muckraking, S.S. McClure, *To Hell in a Day Coach* (Philadelphia, 1968)—properly subtitled "An Exasperated Look At American Railroads"— gives railroad men many deserved knocks. Stewart H. Holbrook's *The Story of American Railroads* (New York, 1947) is his usual well-written and romantic account. However, when it comes to tales of the misdeeds of the "robber barons," no one can compete with Matthew Josephson, *The Robber Barons* (New York, 1934) and Frederick Lewis Allen, *The Lords of Creation* (New York, 1935). Robert G. Lewis's *The Handbook of American Railroads* (New York, 1956) has maps and descriptions which show where and what each of the major (Class I) railroads operated.

There are a series of standard texts which are essential to any study of the railroads. D. Philip Locklin, *Economics of Transportation* (Homewood, Illinois, 1970) is now in its seventh edition. Merle Fainsod, Lincoln Gordon, and Joseph Palamountain, Jr., *Government and the American Economy* (New York, 1959) deserves a fourth edition. I.L. Sharfman, *The Interstate Commerce Commission*, 4 vols. (New York, 1931-7) is the standard, traditional, and highly informational work on the ICC. Robert E. Cushman, *The Independent Regulatory Commissions* (New York, 1941) is the essential history and study of the field, and contains an examination of the British experience as well. Both Sharfman's and Cushman's books were published before World War II.

The modern analytical classic is Marver H. Bernstein, *Regulating Business by Independent Commission* (Princeton, 1955). It should be supplemented by the special March, 1972 number of *The Annals*, which he edited, on "The Government as Regulator." There is a considerable literature on regulatory agencies, of which the most useful are the Oliver Wendell Holmes, Jr. Lectures, given by the noted federal jurist Henry J. Friendly, published in *The Federal Administrative Agencies, The Need for Better Definition of Standards* (Cambridge, 1962), and Roger G. Noll, *Reforming Regulation, An Evaluation of the Asch Council Proposals*, a Brookings Staff Report (Washington, 1971). Louis M. Kohlmeier, Jr., the *Wall Street Journal's* agency expert, has written *The Regulators, Watchdog Agencies and the Public Interest* (New York, 1969), advocating the abolition of the independent commissions, redistribution of some of their functions to the national executive branch, general simplification, and the use of antitrust laws to reestablish competition in a less encumbered marketplace.

The standard and enduring accounts of the Progressive period, which birthed the Hepburn Act, are George Mowry, *The Era of Theodore Roosevelt and the Birth of Modern America* (New York, 1962) and Harold U. Faulkner, *The Decline of Laissez Faire, 1897-1917* (New York, 1951).

There were many investigations of industrial conditions and of the railroads, usually identified by the name of the committee chairman, such as the Windom (1874) and Cullom (1886) reports. Probably the most useful sources on conditions and attitudes during the period in which the regulatory direction was chosen and the Hepburn Act passed are the *Report of the Industrial Commission*, 57th Cong., 1st sess., vols. 9 and 19 (Washington, 1901-1902) and the report of the Senate Interstate Commerce Committee (Elkins committee) *Hearings on Regulation of Railway Rates*, 59th Cong. 1st sess., 5 vols. (Washington, 1905-1906).

The Railroad Problem and the Progressive Era

As "the railroad problem" moved increasingly into the political spotlight during the first decade of the twentieth century, the growth of popular interest was shown by the large number of magazine articles devoted to the subject. *Readers Guide to Periodical Literature* contained eleven columns of article listings in its 1900-1904 volume. The number jumped to thirty-seven columns of listings for the 1905-1909 volume, which covered the period of the battle over the Hepburn Act. This can be compared with the later 1969-1974 volumes, which covered the periods of the rise and fall of Penn Central, of AMTRAK, and the decline of the Northeast railroads, and which contain sixteen columns of listings.

Along with the multivolume Industrial Commission Report, the standard contemporary source on big business in the 1900s was John Moody, *The Truth About The Trusts* (New York, 1904) which contained widely quoted summaries and statistics about each of the nation's four hundred and forty largest corporations. The prime academic railroad authorities were *Railway Legislation in the United States* (New York, 1903), written by Balthasar H. Meyer, a University of Wisconsin professor, who was one of La Follette's first railroad commissioners in Wisconsin and then served on the national ICC for thirty years, and Harvard economics professor William Z. Ripley's *Railway Problems* (Boston, 1907) and *Railroads: Rates and Regulations* (New York, 1912). Chicago political economy professor Hugo R. Meyer, author of *Government Regulation of Railway Rates, A Study of the Experience of the United States, Germany, France, Austria-Hungary, Russia and Australia* (New York, 1905) was a popular witness against government ownership, while Boston University professor and municipal ownership authority Frank Parsons, *The Railways, the Trusts and the People* (Philadelphia, 1905) and *The Heart of the Railroad Problem* (Boston, 1906) was always available to make the argument for nationalization. *The New Encyclopedia of Social Reform*, W.D.P. Bliss, ed. (New York, 1908) summed up the arguments on both sides.

A 1908 symposium, in *The Annals*, vol. 32 (1908), on "The Government and the Railways," contains informative articles on regulation by the various states. Ben Proctor, *Not Without Honor* (Austin, 1962) is a biography of John H. Reagan, who resigned as United States senator to head the Texas Railroad Commission. James F. Doster, *Railroads in Alabama Politics, 1875-1914* (Tuscaloosa, 1957) tells of Alabama Governor Braxton Bragg Comer's unsuccessful struggle against the Louisville & Nashville Railroad.

Because of Robert La Follette's progressive leadership, Wisconsin's regulatory efforts have probably received the most attention. In addition to *La Follette's Autobiography* (Madison, 1913) which is full of excitement, self-praise, and bitterness toward Theodore Roosevelt, the story is told in Robert C. Nesbit, *Wisconsin: A History* (Madison, 1973), one of the best examples of how state history should be written. Herbert F. Margulies, *The Decline of the Progressive Movement in Wisconsin, 1890-1920* (Madison, 1968) tells the La Follette story with insight and balance, while Stanley P. Caine, *The Myth of a Progressive Reform: Railroad Regulation in Wisconsin* (Madison, 1970) convincingly describes the failure of La Follette's most cherished reform.

Harold Woodman, "Chicago Businessmen and the 'Granger' Laws," *Agricultural History*, vol. 36 (January 1962), pp. 16-24; Dale E. Treleven, "Railroads, Elevators, and Grain Dealers: The Genesis of Anti-Monopolism in Milwaukee," *Wisconsin Magazine of History*, vol. 53 (Spring 1969), pp. 205-22; George H. Miller, *Railroads and the Granger Laws* (Madison, 1971); and Lee Benson's modern classic, *Merchants, Farmers & Railroads* (Cambridge, 1955) have led historians to understand the vital role played by shippers and have undercut some of the cliches about the role of angry agrarians in the rise of railroad regulation.

The most important muckraker writings on the railroads are Ida Tarbell, *The History of the Standard Oil Company* (New York, 1904; abridged version, David Chalmers, ed., New York, 1968; Charles Edward Russell, *The Uprising of the Many* (New York, 1907); and Ray Standard Baker, "Railroads on Trial," *McClure's*, vols. 26-27 (1905-1906). David Chalmers, *The Muckrake Years* (New York, 1974) sums up their role.

The able historian of modern large-scale economic organization, Alfred D. Chandler, Jr., author of *The Railroads: The Nation's First Big Business* (New York, 1965) offers an invaluable overview and readings on what was involved in building and running the railroads. Outstanding studies of the attitudes of businessmen are Thomas C. Cochran, *Railroad Leaders 1845-1890: The Business Mind in Action* (Cambridge, 1953) and Edward C. Kirkland, *Dream and Thought in the Business Community, 1860-1900* (Ithaca, 1965). E.G. Campbell, *The Reorganization of the American Railroad System, 1893-1900* (New York, 1938) describes the consolidation movement. Until the much needed major biography of J.P. Morgan comes along, Lewis Corey's critical *The House of Morgan* (New York, 1930) will continue to be the most useful available source. Robert H. Wiebe, *Businessmen and Reform* (Cambridge, 1962) is a first-rate study of the political roles of a less than united business community.

The role of President Roosevelt in the passage of the Hepburn Act is well set forth in William H. Harbaugh, *The Life and Times of Theodore Roosevelt*, ch. 14 (New York, 1961, 1963) and in John Blum, *The Republican Roosevelt* (Cambridge, 1954). No one interested in the topic and the era should miss reading Roosevelt's own writings available in *The Letters of Theodore Roosevelt*, eds. Elting Morison, John Blum, and Alfred Chandler (Cambridge, 1952).

The Battle for the Hepburn Act

Mark Sullivan's *Our Times*, vol. 3, ch. 7 (New York, 1930) tells the story with characteristic zest. In addition to the many studies of Theodore Roosevelt, each of the Senate contestants has his own biography, which adds pieces—and sometimes controversy—to the account. Nathaniel W. Stephenson, *Nelson W. Aldrich, A Leader in American Politics* (New York, 1930) is written in the grand style and sees the Senate struggle as leading to victory for his protagonist. Subsequent historians have disagreed on this and a much needed new biography is being written by Jerome Sternstein. Francis Butler Simkins, *Pitchfork Ben Tillman, South Carolinian* (Baton Rouge, 1944) agrees with Aldrich's biographer, and Tillman, in a generally unfavorable estimation of Roosevelt's role in the struggle. Later biographers Leland L. Sage, author of *William Boyd Allison: A Study in Practical Politics* (Iowa City, 1956), Thomas Richard Ross, who wrote *Jonathan Prentiss Dolliver, A Study in Political Integrity and Independence* (Iowa City, 1958), and Dorothy Ganfield Fowler, biographer of *John Coit Spooner, Defender of Presidents* (New York, 1961) see the Hepburn Act as a victory for reform and offer an approach more in keeping with Blum's and Harbaugh's admiration of

Roosevelt. Ross's *Dolliver* is particularly useful for its account of the senator's leading role in the fight for the railroad rate bill.

Biographies of those such as Nelson W. Aldrich, who fought against the bill is the Senate, John A. Garraty's *Henry Cabot Lodge, A Biography* (New York, 1953), and Everett Walters's, *Joseph Benson Foraker, An Uncompromising Republican* (Columbus, 1948) present their men as not opposed in theory to some limited regulation, but fighting against attempts to make that regulation meaningful. When scholarly biographies now underway on Nelson Aldrich and J.P. Morgan are published, we may learn much more than we presently know about what motivated the leaders of the American business community. However, the basic source for the legislative history of HR 12987 (the Hepburn Act) is the Senate Debates, *Congressional Record*, 59th Cong., 1st sess., February 28-May 18, 1906.

After the Hepburn Act

For the most part, the historians have neglected the post-Hepburn Act story of the American railroads. Overall treatment is to be found only in the latter chapters of the books of John F. Stover and Peter Lyons, and in the economics and regulatory commission texts. Helpful and rare are books such as William G. McAdoo, *The Crowded Years* (Boston, 1931) and Walker D. Hines, *War History of the American Railroads* (New Haven, 1928) which provide accounts of their World War stewardship of the nationalized railroads, and Claude Fuess, *Joseph B. Eastman, Servant of the People* (New York, 1952), describing Eastman's role as he moved from Boston's Public Franchise League, to the Massachusetts Public Service Commission, to the Interstate Commerce Commission, Federal Coordinator of Transportation during the depression, and then to become World War II Director of Defense Transportation.

The Annual Reports of the Interstate Commerce Commission provide summary statistics and very brief comment on the general status of the railroads. Philadelphia *Bulletin* newsmen Joseph R. Daughen and Peter Binzen have written an account of *The Wreck of the Penn Central* (Boston, 1971). Further information on the ups and downs—mostly the latter—of the railroads is to be found in Rush Loving, Jr., "A Costly Rescue for the Northeast Railroads," *Fortune*, vol. 89 (February, 1974), pp. 118-22, and "Amtrak is About to Miss the Train," *Fortune*, vol. 89 (May, 1974), pp. 272-90; in Joseph Albright, "A hell of a way to run a government," New York *Times Magazine* (November 3, 1974), p. 16ff; and in the *Congressional Quarterly, Business Week*, and the *Wall Street Journal*. The findings of a government study, commissioned by the Council of Economic Advisors and the National Commission on Productivity, are summed up by its directors in John R. Meyer and Alexander L. Morton, "A better way to run the railroads," *Harvard Business Review*, vol. 52 (July-August, 1974), pp. 141-48.

Bright spots in what has otherwise been the recent disinterest in railroad history, have been the powerful free-market arguments of Albro Martin, and the New Left critiques of Gabriel Kolko and those who have been influenced by him. In his prize-winning *Enterprise Denied, Origins of the Decline of American Railroads, 1897-1917* (New York, 1971) and "The Troubled Subject of Railroad Regulation in the Gilded Age—A Reappraisal," *The Journal of American History*, vol. 61 (September, 1974), Martin argues that enterpriser pooling or consolidation, rather than inept regulation, was what the railroads needed in order to stay healthy. In his footnotes and text, he offers stern comment on other railroad studies, including Gabriel Kolko's.

In his prize-winning *Railroads and Regulation, 1877-1916* (New York, 1965) and his later written but earlier published *The Triumph of*

Conservatism, A Reinterpretation of American History, 1900-1916 (New York, 1963), Gabriel Kolko offers a heavily documented argument that regulation was not antibusiness reform, but that business used politics to extend its market control. Kolko calls this "political capitalism" and offers a strong case for the contention that the regulatory commissions and agencies have been part of the business "community of interest."

Kolko's attack on the traditional interpretation of reform has helped stimulate historical investigation of the origins and meaning of the American regulatory experience. James Weinstein, *The Corporate Ideal in the Liberal State: 1900-1918* (Boston, 1968) joins Kolko's analysis of the business origins of government regulation.

Edward A. Purcell, Jr., "Ideas and Interests: Businessmen and the Interstate Commerce Act," *Journal of American History*, vol. 65 (December, 1967), pp. 561-78; Robert W. Harbeson, "Railroads and Regulation, 1877-1916: Conspiracy or Public Interest?" *Journal of Economic History*, vol. 27 (June, 1967), pp. 230-42; and K. Austin Kerr, *American Railroad Politics, 1914-1920, Rates, Wages, and Efficiency* (Pittsburgh, 1968) are praiseworthy examples of the stimulus that new interpretations, controversy, and rigorous scholarship provide.